# THINGS EVERY PHOTOGRAPHER SHOULD KNOW

Mastering Composition, Lighting, Lenses, Focus, Editing, Posing, Storytelling, Color Theory, Exposure, and Much More!

## Cole Nelson

# FREE BONUS

## SCAN TO GET OUR NEXT BOOK FOR FREE!

# Table of Contents

# INTRODUCTION

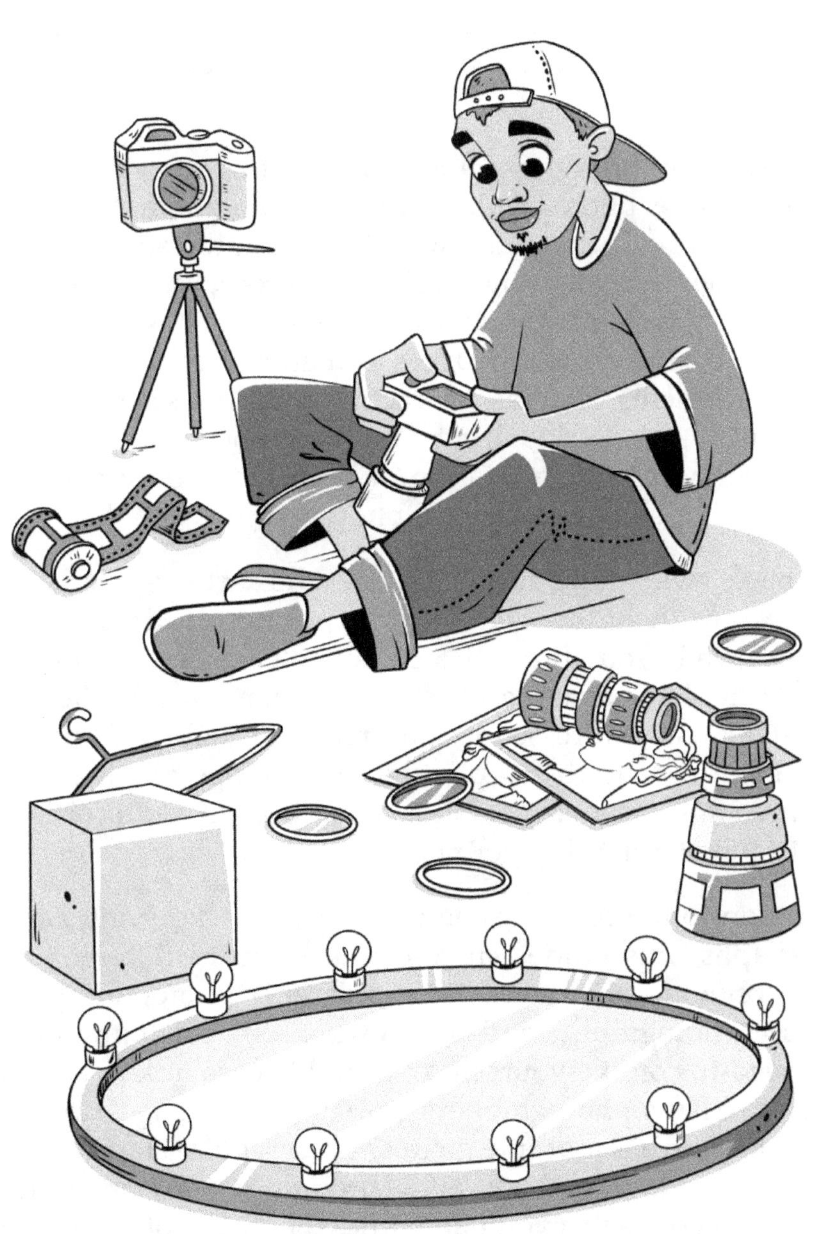

Since its invention in the early 19th century, photography has been an essential means of documenting the world and the people, places, and things that comprise it. With the advent of the handheld camera and then the smartphone, people of all ages have been able to experiment with photography, making this arguably one of the most commonly used creative mediums in the world.

As you will see throughout this book, photography is both an art and a science. A photograph captures the photographer's unique viewpoint, providing a window into their interests, preferences, and priorities. When done well, a photograph can convey a compelling message to the viewer. In this way, it is an individual form of art. However, this art is sometimes based on complex technical elements, such as interacting with the science of vision and light. As an aspiring photographer, you need an understanding and appreciation of both the science and the art that together make up successful photography.

This book will introduce you to the artistic elements of photography, including composition, posing, and color theory. It will also walk you through technical elements such as lenses, depth of field, exposure, and focusing techniques. While each of these will be addressed separately throughout this book, remember that successful photography brings all these factors together simultaneously; you will think as both artist and scientist when practicing your craft.

In addition to the basic strategies needed for capturing beautiful photographs, this guide will introduce you to different genres within photography, such as landscape photography, long-exposure photography, and portraiture. As a photographer, you don't need to confine yourself to a single genre unless you prefer to do so. Many photographers pursue their images in diverse settings and across multiple genres. When you're starting out, it's a good idea to try them all. Through experimentation and experience, you will eventually find the types of photography that most appeal to you and your artistic vision.

It's worth noting that while their general functionality is the same, all cameras are slightly different. The information provided in this book is designed to be broad enough to apply when using any brand or model of camera. However, this book shouldn't be used in isolation. It's important to read the manual that came with your camera so that you can learn any special functions or features that are unique to your brand and model.

The best way to use this book is to read each chapter as a whole and take plenty of time to practice all the techniques before moving onto the next chapter. For example, make sure you've practiced the various focusing techniques described here until you feel comfortable with each of them. By mastering each chapter's contents before moving onto the next, your knowledge and skills in photography can grow exponentially. Furthermore, the material here is strategically arranged so that each successive chapter will build upon the ones that came before.

# [1]
# THE POWER OF COMPOSITION

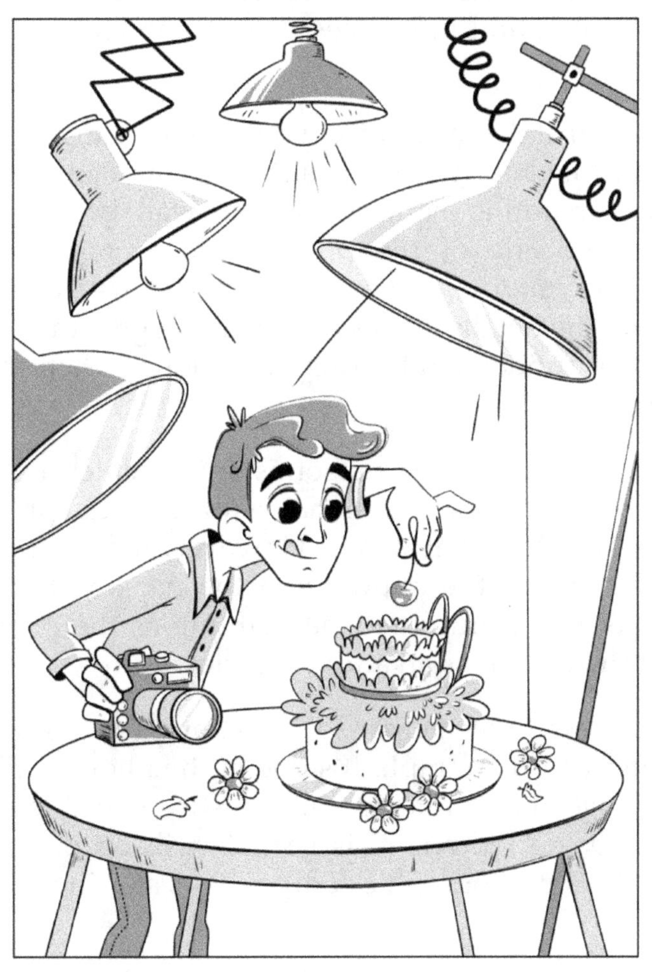

Composition is one of the most fundamental aspects of compelling, beautiful, and effective photography. In the realm of photography, *composition* refers to the layout of content within a photo. This content may be direct subjects, like the people or objects you're photographing, but it can also include backgrounds, landscapes, props, and other incidentals that are captured within the frame. A powerful photo balances each of these elements and ensures they're placed within the photo in a way that draws the viewer in. Composition also helps to direct the viewer's focus and influences them to understand the image in a particular way.

Each time you take a photo, you're capturing a particular composition. Maybe a person is sitting on a chair in the center, but there's a painting hanging on the wall behind them and toward the left side of the photo. This arrangement—seated person in the middle, painting to the left—is the photo's composition. The details of this arrangement give the viewer cues to help them understand your intentions when taking the photograph.

In this case, since the seated person is in the center, most viewers will interpret that person as the main subject of the photo and the painting as an additional detail. However, if you took a photo with the painting in the middle and the person off to the side, then a viewer might interpret the painting as the photo's actual subject and the person as an additional detail.

This simple example helps to illustrate the importance of composition in a photograph. It's one of the photographer's tools for conveying their intentions, artistic style, and unique perspective to the viewer. This section will cover some of the fundamentals of photographic composition, starting with the rule of thirds.

# RULE OF THIRDS

The rule of thirds is an easy-to-remember mathematical trick for balancing composition within a photograph. It serves as a way to ensure that the entire frame of a photograph is interesting and balanced, which ultimately creates a more impactful image.

The rule of thirds requires the photographer to imagine the photo they intend to take before they actually take it. When looking through the viewfinder, the photographer should imagine that the image is divided into a grid of nine blocks. This can be achieved by envisioning three vertical lines evenly spaced across the image and three horizontal lines evenly spaced up and down. When these lines are in place, the image is divided into a grid of nine equally sized rectangles. In many cases, you as the photographer are only imagining this grid across your image. However, some cameras allow you to apply that grid when looking through the viewfinder so that you can actually see the nine blocks dividing your image.

The rule of thirds dictates that important elements in a photo should be positioned along one of those imaginary lines or at one of the places the lines intersect. The closer each of the objects in the photo is to one of those lines or intersections, the more balanced the photo will appear.

Without applying the rule of thirds, you may end up with photos that have one item of interest in the center and nothing on either side. While this is a simple, effective strategy for casual photography, you'll want to balance elements of interest throughout the frame to achieve a more professional and artistic approach.

# LEADING LINES

As compositional features, leading lines direct the viewer's eye toward the main subject. These lines can be straight, but they don't have to be; they can curve or even converge within the frame. Leading lines are made of elements within the photo itself. For example, if you take a photo of a friend standing next to a long fence, the top of that fence may provide a visual line that leads the viewer to look at your friend.

Of course, not every photograph is taken next to a fence, along a road, or near something that happens to be linear in shape. This is why it's important to embrace your creativity when photographing. A singular line of light or even a shadow can serve as a leading line. Leading lines can be bold or very subtle as long as they serve to keep the viewer's attention focused on the main subject of the photograph.

# FRAMING

Like a wooden picture frame that provides a visual boundary for a printed photo or piece of art, a frame *within* a photo provides a visual boundary that keeps the viewer's eye on the photo's main subject. Imagine it as a picture frame within your picture, providing a border around what you think is most important for the viewer to see.

A simple example would be taking a picture of a friend who's standing in a doorway. The shape of the doorway frames your subject, so it's clear the viewer is meant to look at them. Taking pictures through open doors and windows is a great framing option, as is taking a picture through the branches of trees.

In addition to bordering your main subject, framing can help provide a sense of scale and proportion within a photo. For example, if you take a picture of a car that's some distance away on a flat road with nothing around it, it will be difficult for your viewer to perceive the size of the car. However, if you photograph the car while it's passing under an overhang of leafy tree branches, those branches can frame the car and provide your viewer another reference point.

Rather than leaving your subject isolated in the photo, experiment with ways to frame that subject using objects, architecture, the natural world, and even light, shading, and texture. Be creative! If you're photographing your dog on the beach, don't just take a picture of the dog on the sand. Instead, draw a shape in the sand and put your dog inside it. The outlined shape will provide a frame for your subject—the dog—and will make the photo look more finished and interesting.

# SYMMETRY AND PATTERNS

The concepts of symmetry and patterns are undoubtedly familiar to you. These are concepts many of us first learned in art class as children, and unlike the rule of thirds or leading lines, these terms are commonly used in daily life. This familiarity will be helpful as you get used to the way both symmetry and patterns are used in photography.

*Symmetry* refers to an image or object where one side is the mirror image of the other. For example, if you draw a perfect circle on a paper, that circle is symmetrical. If you divide it down the middle, each half is the mirror image of the other. On the other hand, a drawing of a crescent moon is not symmetrical. If you divide it down the middle, the lines making up the moon on the left would not match those on the right.

Studies have shown that humans prefer viewing objects that are symmetrical. There is even evidence to suggest that perfectly symmetrical faces are perceived as more attractive than those that are asymmetrical. There is something satisfying about symmetry, and it's likely to be pleasing or calming to a viewer. While these are generally considered to be positive attributes, as a photographer, you might prefer to create images that are unique, intriguing, exciting, or thought provoking. Thus, you might seek to avoid symmetry in your photos, as there is no rule stating that a great photograph must be symmetrical. Instead, symmetry and asymmetry are strategies you can use to help create the photo—and viewer experience—that you seek.

Repeating patterns create visual interest and may hold your viewer's attention for longer. Humans are naturally drawn to patterns, especially those they find especially interesting or attractive. You can create patterns in your photos by seeking a repetition of specific elements, such as tall trees spaced evenly across the frame or alternating colors in the background. Creative and strategic uses of patterns according to your own style and preferences may create photos that are more interesting and engaging for your viewers.

# [2]
# MASTERING
# EXPOSURE

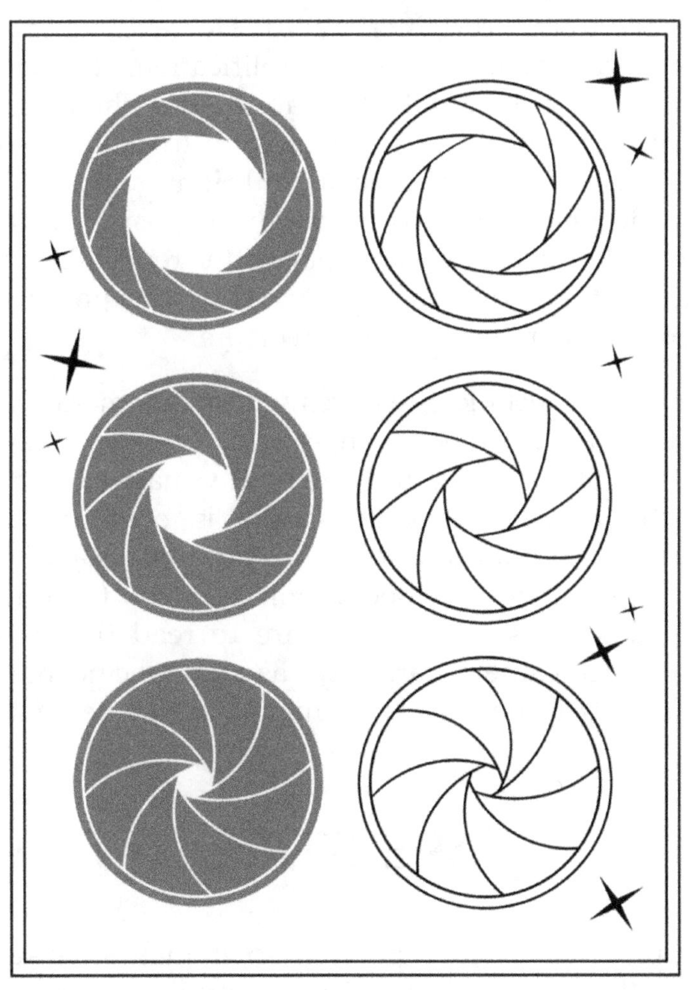

In photography, exposure refers to the amount of light captured by the camera in a particular photograph. A great deal of photography comes down to controlling and manipulating light in your photos, so exposure is a crucial element to master. The word *expose* generally means "to make visible." Since photography is all about viewing, it's not surprising that mastering the visibility of your subject is at the core of this idea.

A low level of exposure results in a darker photo, while a high exposure results in a brighter photo. However, there is much more to exposure than this oversimplification. In photography, too much light or not enough can lead to poor photos. Over time, you'll learn to balance levels of exposure to achieve effects like dramatic shadows in an otherwise bright shot or bursts of highlights despite a cloudy sky. By exposing your photos effectively, you can create ones that better replicate the nuances of natural sight, or you can experiment with exposure to create heightened drama in the images you create.

There are several technical features within a camera that control and adjust exposure levels. As an aspiring photographer, it's vital that you learn to navigate, and eventually master, each one. The basic functionality of these elements is common across all cameras, so it's important to build an understanding of the mechanics of a camera. This book will help you to do that. Once you understand these basics, be sure to read the manual that came with your camera carefully, as the specific buttons and knobs that control these features may differ somewhat between models.

# APERTURE

An aperture is a hole or opening, so it makes sense that the aperture of the camera is the circle through which a picture is taken. An aperture is like the pupil in your eye: a round opening that controls the amount of light that enters.

When pupils dilate, they become larger and let in more light. For example, at dusk or in a darkened room, your pupil will dilate to allow in as much light as possible to see. Alternatively, your pupils can constrict when they want to reduce the amount of light that gets in. If you're outside on a very sunny day, your pupils will constrict to prevent too much light from getting through.

The aperture on your camera has the exact same functionality. The aperture is surrounded by overlapping plates, or blades, typically made of plastic, that can constrict or expand. Many cameras will do this automatically, but as a photographer, you can manually make these adjustments to create the light effect you're seeking.

The extent to which a camera aperture is open or shut is quantifiable. This means that you can name the aperture you're using or make notes of the effects you're able to achieve with different settings. Apertures are expressed as fractions in the format f/#. For example, an aperture may be f/2 or f/16. Think of these as fractions: 1/2 or 1/16. As you know, 1/2 is larger than 1/8 or 1/16. Likewise, f/2 is larger than f/8 or f/16. While the smallest aperture you can likely achieve is f/32, depending on your camera, the largest could go up to f/1.4 or even f/0.8.

Remember that the larger your aperture, the more light gets in. Experiment with using larger apertures at dusk or indoors and smaller apertures outside on bright days. By trying various apertures and examining the results, you will start to note the aperture's impact.

# SHUTTER SPEED

Another function that determines the amount of light that will enter your camera is shutter speed. While aperture controls light through the size of the camera's lens opening, shutter speed controls light by determining how long the camera spends taking a picture. The longer the shutter speed, the more time light is entering your camera and the brighter your picture will be.

Shutter speed is measured in time. It might be 1/10 of a second or 1/100 of a second. The longest shutter speed on most cameras is about 30 seconds, and novelty cameras have been built with shutter speeds of years, or even decades, to capture a single photo!

For your purposes, you probably won't need to worry about years-long or even minutes-long shutter speeds. Rather, you'll want to focus on the difference between short shutter speeds and how they enable you to control the level of light in your photographs.

Shutter speed is not only useful for adjusting light levels, but it can also be used to capture a sense of motion in photography when used effectively. When used ineffectively, that motion can look like a distracting blur. While a long shutter speed allows more time for light to enter the camera, it also allows more time for your subject to move.

If you're trying to take a photo of a child smiling, you might want to do it quickly; otherwise, the child will likely fidget, and the image will blur. However, if you want to capture a sense of the wind in the trees, then allowing a bit of that movement or blur to enter the image might not be a bad thing. Keep in mind that when you use a longer shutter speed, you are doing so with intention and being thoughtful about whether and why you want to allow blur in your image.

# ISO

ISO, or ISO sensitivity, is another tool at your disposal when you need to control or adjust for light in an image. Both aperture and shutter speed control for light mechanically by physically determining the amount of light able to enter the camera. ISO, however, allows you to brighten your photos within the camera itself after the camera has been exposed to outside light.

ISO is a setting that you can adjust. It exists along a scale with main stops at 100, 200, 400, 800, 1600, 3200, and 6400. The larger the number, the brighter the resulting image. It may be tempting to set your ISO in the middle to high range to ensure that your photos are always bright enough. However, don't give in to this temptation.

The clearest, most natural-looking photos are usually achieved by setting your camera to its lowest ISO (called the "base ISO") while using aperture and shutter speed to expose the photo properly. Using ISO to brighten an under-exposed image may seem helpful, but it can distort the colors in the image and make the objects in the photo appear grainy or pixelated. A photo that is distorted in this way is often called a "noisy" photo, and you usually want to avoid the grainy, color-changed appearance that is associated with "noise" in photography. Experiment with ISO but remember that a properly exposed photo is still your best bet.

In some cases, when you're dealing with extremely low light, you may find that it's impossible to get enough light into your photo. This is when ISO really comes in handy. Increasing your ISO may still create a noisy photo, but that may be better than one that is almost entirely dark.

# UNDERSTANDING THE EXPOSURE TRIANGLE

You've learned about aperture, shutter speed, and ISO, each of which functions to control the amount of light or brightness in your photo. These three concepts work together to produce images, and you can think of them as cooperative partners in your photographic process.

Picture an equilateral triangle where each side is the same length. Imagine that aperture, shutter speed, and ISO each make up one side. This is the "exposure triangle." The three sides of the exposure triangle need to work together and remain perfectly balanced in order for the triangle to maintain its shape. If one side changes, the others must change as well to keep the same balance.

Basically, as you adjust one element of exposure on your camera, you'll need to adjust the others as well. A larger aperture may require a shorter shutter speed to keep the light balanced. A longer shutter speed may work best with a lower ISO to avoid overexposure. Experiment with these three elements so that you can achieve the optimal exposure for the photo you intend to take.

# [3]
# THE IMPORTANCE
# OF LIGHTING

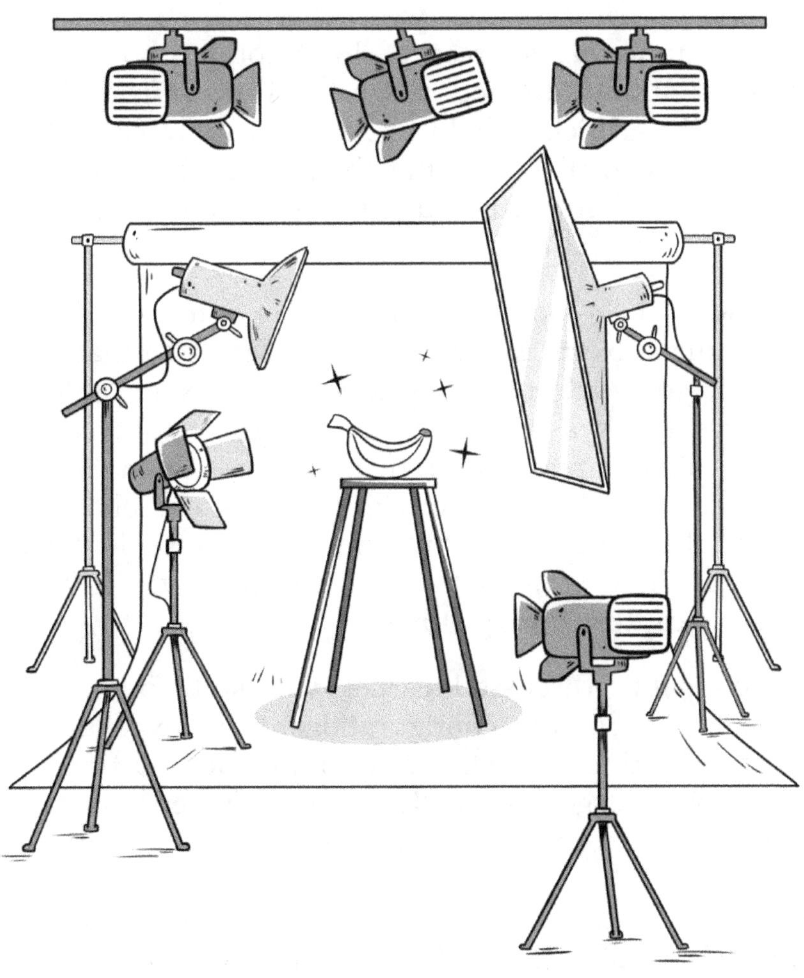

As you've already gleaned from the sections above, effective lighting is a crucial component of successful photography. Regardless of the subject you've chosen for your photo—maybe a professional's head shot, an action photo of a sports team, or an architectural shoot of a new building—light itself is always a secondary subject in each photo you take. You cannot take a photo without light, so whether you know it or not, you are always taking a picture *of* light as well, and it's important to learn to use it to your advantage.

There are numerous sources of light for a photograph, and they're most simply divided into natural or artificial light. Both natural and artificial light sources can create beautiful photographs, so neither is better than the other. You'll learn to work differently with each and perhaps come to prefer one over the other.

Regardless of the type of lighting you're using, you'll need to position your subjects thoughtfully in relation to that light. For example, if your subject is positioned in between you and the light source (such as a person standing in front of a bright window while you photograph them from inside the room), they may appear only in silhouette with their features obscured. This is because the light is behind them. In contrast, if the light is behind you while you photograph a subject, you'll be able to more clearly capture their features.

The functionality discussed earlier will still come into play. Experiment with various configurations of the exposure triangle in different lighting contexts. For example, do you find that you rely more on a larger or smaller aperture when indoors under artificial light? Are you more likely to maximize ISO adjustments only under either indoor or outdoor conditions? By understanding and experimenting with all these factors together, you'll develop a stronger understanding of your camera and the broadest possible set of photographic skills.

# NATURAL LIGHT

Natural light refers to light that comes from natural sources. In most cases, this natural light source is the sun, though in some cases the moon or even the stars provide enough light for taking effective images at night.

It might seem intuitive to associate natural light photos with being outdoors but remember this isn't necessarily the case. Rooms with skylights, large windows, or direct sun exposure provide more than enough natural light for photography, so you can plan photos with natural light in both indoor and outdoor environments.

One thing to remember when working with natural light is that it will constantly change, subtly but perceptibly. If you've planned an hour-long photo shoot with a client, the angle of the sun will differ considerably at the start and end of that shoot. As the photographer, you will need to plan accordingly. This is particularly true if your photo session is scheduled for around sunrise or sunset when the light tends to change the fastest. As you build more experience in your craft, you'll become better able to predict the changing amount, tone, and angle of natural light through the days and seasons.

Using natural light in photography offers several benefits, including the fact that it's freely available! However, it brings challenges as well, one of which is its variability. Natural lighting conditions will be impacted by your latitude and altitude, the setting of your photograph, the time of day, and the time of year. Despite all those variables, there are some general rules of thumb to keep in mind when shooting in natural light for all photographers.

First, remember that light from above—for example, under the noon sun or directly under a skylight—will create harsh shadows across your subject. Lighting that comes from directly above can be harder to work with than light that comes from an angle, so plan your locations and photography schedule carefully with this in mind.

When you have a light source that comes from an angle, try to ensure that your subject faces toward the light, rather than away from it, if you want to capture their features. Light will illuminate and clarify the surface it touches first, while leaving other surfaces shadowed or somewhat obscured. This means that if you're taking a portrait of a person, they should be positioned with their face toward the light source to ensure you can capture them clearly.

# ARTIFICIAL LIGHT

Artificial light comes from any source besides the sun, moon, and stars. Artificial light sources are incredibly diverse, and learning to identify and master them will add a range of new photographic opportunities to your repertoire.

When photographing with artificial light, which usually means photographing indoors, be alert to possible light sources. Overhead lights and table and desk lamps are obvious choices in casual environments, just like standing flashes are familiar in professional photography settings. However, it's important to pay attention to less obvious sources of light as well. For example, consider the way a tablet screen lights up the face of its user, creating enough light for a photograph of that user's face. The small lights in a fish tank might be enough to take a beautiful photo of the tank's occupants. A light doesn't need to be large or powerful to be enough for a photograph as long as you've mastered the exposure triangle and composition.

As the aforementioned examples illustrate, there are numerous light sources in indoor environments. While this is visually interesting and appealing to viewers in that environment, a mixture of different light sources can create problems in a photograph. Each light source brings its own intensity and tone, or white balance, and combining those can interfere with a photo's exposure. Whenever possible, try to limit your environment to just one artificial light source during a photography session. By using just one light source, you can better control your exposure and the photographic outcome.

You may find that you need to increase your ISO and/or your aperture when shooting indoors with artificial light. Experiment until you find what works best.

# GOLDEN HOUR

The "golden hour" (also called the "magic hour") refers to the last hour before sunset and the first hour right after sunrise. These times of day are known for their dramatic light effects, and they are the most popular times for outdoor photo shoots.

There are a few characteristics of light during this time that make it special and uniquely suited to beautiful photography. The section on natural light addressed the fact that the quality, amount, and tone of sunlight shift throughout the day, and it is those characteristic shifts that make golden-hour light so appealing.

Light during the golden hour comes in from an angle near the horizon rather than from directly overhead like at midday. This angled light is softer and more diffuse, which typically creates a more flattering effect for photography subjects. Soft lighting helps to even out skin tones, for example, and avoids harsh shadows that can be unflattering. An additional benefit is that it is difficult to accidentally overexpose an image during the golden hour. The softness of the light lends itself to photography and is relatively easy to balance in a photo.

The angle of light during the golden hour also creates some appealing dramatic effects like long shadows and sunbursts.

These elements can infuse an emotional or nostalgic sense in a photo that might not emerge in harsh lighting.

Finally, golden-hour light is warm along the color temperature spectrum as opposed to being cool. This warm light contains yellow, orange, and red undertones and filters out blue tones. The effect of this is a color palette that people tend to associate with happiness and warmth, again enhancing the emotional effect of photos taken at these times of day.

With all these appeals of the golden hour, you might be eager to get out there and start taking some photos as the sun goes down. However, keep in mind that the golden hour also brings some challenges. Chief among these is that it's over quickly: it really is just an hour at the start and end of the day. A photographer needs to work quickly during the golden hour. It's a good idea to plan your shoots ahead of time so that you don't have to worry about setting up or choosing your angles and backdrops.

When photographing during golden hour, one tip is to take plenty of photos, more than you might at other times of day. The light changes so quickly during this time of day that it's a good idea to capture as many versions as possible. You never know which one will come out truly magical.

# CONTROLLING SHADOWS

With all the focus on light thus far, it's easy to overlook the importance of shadows in photography—specifically, the photographer's ability to control shadows in an image. As mentioned above, the golden hour creates long, dramatic shadows that can be appealing in a photo. However, those shadows can also throw off the balance of an image, creating large dark spaces that the photographer didn't necessarily want.

Shadows will inevitably be present in the photographs you take, so it's essential to learn how to use them to your advantage.

When preparing to take a photo, always take a moment to consider the shadows you might have overlooked. Make sure no shadows exist across parts of your subject that you intend to expose and make adjustments to lighting and angles as needed to keep your subject in the light and reduce those troublesome shadows. While increasing your ISO will brighten up unintended shadows, it will also brighten the image as a whole.

Some photographers take the opposite approach and purposefully focus on the shadows in their images. Shadow photography, in which the photographs are of the shadows themselves or using the shadows in intentional ways to create a visual effect, is an interesting area to explore as you hone your craft.

# [4]
# GETTING TO KNOW YOUR CAMERA

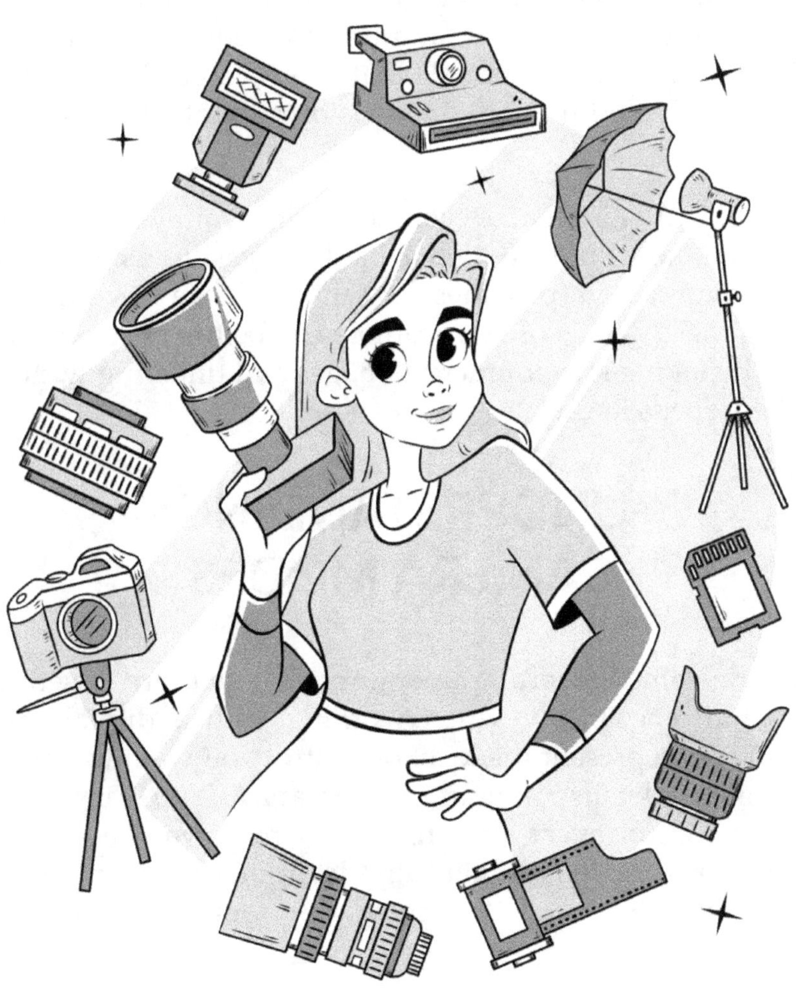

As you've learned about aspects like shutter speed, aperture, and ISO, you've begun to build familiarity with the basic functionality of your camera. This next section of the book will build upon that with topics such as common camera modes, customized settings, and manual versus automatic photography.

Each camera offers these general features, so all the information in this section should apply regardless of your camera's make and model. However, remember that each camera may have slightly different controls. In addition to reading the information provided here, it's essential that you carefully review the instructions (including online videos or tutorials) that came with your camera.

You'll need to familiarize yourself with your camera's focus modes and how to shift between them easily, as well as the options your camera provides for white balance in your images. Learning these details of your camera can be fun. The best way to do so is by taking lots of practice images and tinkering with white balance or focus in each.

# UNDERSTANDING CAMERA MODES

There are some general camera modes that are essential to understand, specifically when working with a digital camera. These modes represent the level of control you want to have over the technical details of your photography. You may want to manually control every option, or you may want the camera's internal computer to automatically determine and apply some of those options for you. You may even opt for something in between.

Depending on your goals for the photo you're taking, you can decide which mode makes the most sense. Shifting between modes is typically a quick and easy process, so you may find that you utilize multiple modes among your shots in a single photo session.

Your camera may have what is called a PASM or PASM dial. This is a round dial that you can turn to adjust the camera's mode, and its name comes from the letters *P*, *S*, *A*, and *M* displayed prominently on the dial. These stand for *program, shutter priority, aperture priority*, and *manual*. If your camera doesn't have a physical dial with these settings, you may adjust the mode through its digital screen instead.

# MANUAL VS. AUTOMATIC

Many beginner or casual photographers aren't interested in learning or mastering the technical functionality of their camera. They may just want reassurance that the images they capture will be clear with appropriate lighting and color tones. For these photographers, program mode (also known as automatic mode) makes sense. Program mode leaves all the technical decisions up to the camera, depending on the light, angles, shadows, and other aspects that it can sense automatically. In program mode, your camera will adjust things like aperture automatically to capture the default amount of light it has been programmed to prefer. In most cases, this will result in a perfectly decent photo.

On the other end of the spectrum, manual mode gives the photographer full control over all the technical decision-making that goes into the photographic process. For example, you'll direct the camera's shutter speed and aperture so that you can fine tune every image you take. This mode is ideal when you have a specific goal in mind, one that you may be able to achieve through making your own adjustments.

In between program and manual modes, your camera may offer aperture and/or shutter priority modes. Aperture priority mode allows you to control your aperture to determine precisely how much light you want to allow into an image, but the camera will determine the shutter speed automatically. Shutter priority mode is the opposite. You control your shutter speed manually, while the camera determines the appropriate aperture for you.

# CUSTOMIZING SETTINGS

With this basic understanding of the modes available to you on most cameras, you may wonder when a photographer should use each of these. The answer is that there is no simple right or wrong when it comes to which setting you'll choose. As with other elements of photography, you will determine the settings you prefer in different situations based on practice and experimentation over time. Let's discuss examples of when you might want to try out one or more of these modes as a place to begin your exploration of different camera settings.

Program mode allows the photographer to take pictures quickly and easily so that they can focus on what's happening around them rather than concentrating too much on the process of photography itself. If you're enjoying a performance by your favorite band, informally capturing a child's birthday, or taking a quick shot while at dinner with friends, then program mode should serve your purposes well. You can rely on a reasonably clear, natural-looking photograph without having to spend time posing your subjects, adjusting them relative to the light, or fiddling with your settings. Program mode is your go-to mode for everyday photography.

Aperture priority mode often comes in handy, particularly when taking photos in very low or high light. Even if you're in one of those casual settings and looking to capture a no-frills picture, using program mode at dusk or in a very bright setting may result in a picture that's disappointingly under- or overexposed.

In these cases, it's worth taking a moment or two to manually adjust your aperture to control the light exposure of your shot and hopefully achieve the best result.

Shutter priority will be useful when your goal is to capture action shots, such as at a soccer match or dance recital. In these cases, you want to capture the sense of movement without a distorted blur that distracts from the details of the photo. Leverage your knowledge of different shutter speeds to determine the one that will best fit your purposes. Shutter priority will allow you to make that decision about shutter speed (or even try the pictures with several different shutter speeds) without having to worry about adjusting lighting/aperture as well.

Finally, manual mode is your best bet under very difficult photography situations, such as those that are action packed and dimly lit. It's also ideal when you want to focus on your craft and create an image that is original, artistic, or otherwise reflects your personal style as the photographer. By taking all the technical controls into your own hands, you can play with exposure and shutter speed to create a photo that best reflects your goals as a photographer. Manual mode gives you the most control for how you'd like a photo to come out, so when you have the time and ability to concentrate on your photography, this is likely the mode you'll turn to frequently.

# READING THE HISTOGRAM

You may remember the term *histogram* from school. A histogram is a graph that visually represents the distribution of data. In other words, it shows how frequently a different condition appears. It looks similar to a bar chart but without any gaps or spaces in between the individual bars.

A digital camera will provide you with a luminosity histogram on its screen whenever you have the camera turned on and focused on an image. Rather than looking like bars, the histogram will probably look like a curve on the graph, perhaps in the shape of a mountain range, before dropping down to the horizontal axis at each end.

In the case of photography, the luminosity histogram represents levels of brightness in your image. The far left of the histogram nearest the vertical axis represents pure black, while the far right represents pure white (total brightness) in the image. Since we don't—and can't—photograph pure white or pure black and expect a meaningful image to result, those ends of the graph are typically at the horizontal axis, representing a value of zero.

The space in between those extremes represents all the different tones of light in your image, and this is the part you'll use to interpret what you're seeing. It takes some practice to interpret the histogram effectively. For example, you may notice that when the histogram is concentrated in the middle, or any small area, this results in an image that lacks contrast. In other words, you won't notice a lot of difference between the light and the shadow in the photo. This is because the histogram is telling you that all the light tones are bunched up in a small range without the wider spread that would represent a broader range of tones.

Get in the habit of viewing that histogram during your photography sessions, and experiment with the results when you take photos with differing luminosity histograms.

# [5]
# FOCUSING TECHNIQUES

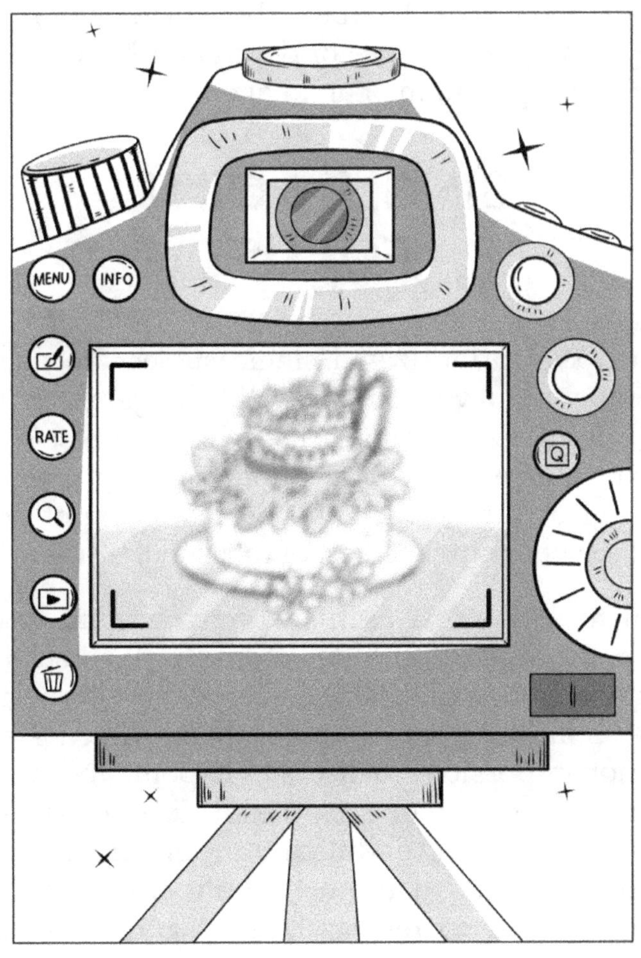

While light and exposure are key ingredients to any successful photograph, they are not the only concepts involved. You are likely already familiar with the concept of *focus* in photography, and mastering your camera's various approaches to focus will be the next step to further developing your craft.

*Focus* refers to the crispness and clarity of the image you intend to shoot. Most digital cameras take care of focus automatically, so for many amateur photographers, focus is something they're aware of but don't actively think about. However, using focus strategically can create a sense of depth and have a huge impact on a viewer's interpretation of an image.

# SINGLE-POINT FOCUS

Single-point focus prioritizes a single subject, focusing on one specific point within your frame. With single-point focus, that subject will be in clear, crisp focus, while the rest of the frame may be more blurred. If you're photographing a trophy that a team just won or the new kitten you just brought home, those subjects will be your single object of focus in the frame.

Single-point focus is most useful when you want to emphasize that single point of focus and de-emphasize the background. It's especially useful when the subject is reasonably static and they're going to stay still for the photo rather than be in constant motion. While it's not impossible to use single-point focus on moving subjects, because this mode is meant to provide detail and precision, it's much more difficult to maintain that level of specificity on a subject that is constantly changing. You would need to be prepared to refocus quickly and often in order to attempt this type of shot.

If you are seeking precision in your photography, single-point focus can be the best way to achieve that. With single-point focus, you tell the camera exactly where to direct its attention in order to deliver the clearest, crispest results. On many cameras, single-point focus will happen automatically whenever there is a clear subject in the frame; this is referred to as single-point autofocus, or single point AF. You also have the option of defining your single-point focus manually if you want to focus on a subject other than what your camera identifies automatically.

# CONTINUOUS FOCUS

In contrast to single point AF, continuous focus is intended for photographing subjects in motion. This mode is automatically programmed within digital cameras so that you as the photographer aren't required to keep up with frequent shifts in focus. In this mode, your camera will track the moving subject, such as a dog running towards you, and refocus as needed to adjust for that motion and the dog's distance from the camera. In theory, whenever you click the shutter to capture an image, the camera will be appropriately focused on the subject at that moment in time.

Since this mode requires the camera to constantly recheck its subject and refocus as needed, you'll want to confirm that it's focused prior to taking a picture. If you happen to take the photo while the camera is in the process of refocusing, or just before it has adjusted to your moving subject, then you'll end up with a blurry image as a result.

Different cameras have different ways of telling you when they're focused and ready to shoot. For example, some will illuminate a colored light whenever they are in focus, and that colored light will disappear temporarily while the camera is in the process of focusing again. In that case, you want to be sure to take your picture only when the light is illuminated. Familiarize yourself with the continuous focus mode of your individual camera, and make sure you know how to determine whether or not the camera is focused before you shoot.

Keep in mind that continuous focus mode is not perfect and will not always track your subject accurately. It works best with a subject that is moving predictably at a set pace, but it may struggle with a subject that speeds up or slows down. Unpredictable subjects are particularly hard to photograph in focus, as neither you nor your camera know exactly where they're about to go.

# MANUAL FOCUS

In manual focus mode, all the decisions about where to focus within the frame are up to you. In general, most photographers use autofocus more often than manual focus simply for convenience. Autofocus, whether manual or continuous, allows you to take your photos quickly and provides a reasonable assurance of clarity. In fact, autofocus may provide a greater level of accuracy in the result than manual focus.

However, it is only through manual focus that you can fully understand and master the use of your camera. While your camera is capable of focusing on your behalf, you may want the flexibility to experiment with different methods of focusing in your images. For example, you may want to intentionally create a blurry image to produce a cloudy or dreamy effect. To do so, you would need to manually override your camera's automatic focus.

There are also some situations in which manual focus is likely to outperform the camera's automatic capabilities, such as in situations with low light or when focusing on a subject very close to the camera. You will also likely utilize manual focus when you want to focus on just one of multiple subject options in the frame. For example, you may be taking a picture of two people standing side by side, but you may want to prioritize the focus on just one of them and not the other. Your camera would not easily be able to do this in automatic mode, as it would not know which of the subjects to choose. In this case, your ability to manually direct the focus is essential to the photographic goal you're pursuing.

# DEPTH OF FIELD

Alongside focus and exposure, depth of field is one of photography's most important concepts because it helps direct the viewer's eye to the part of the photograph you want them to notice. By prioritizing certain areas of focus and choosing the parts that appear blurry or out of focus, you're telling the viewers what to see in it.

The concept of depth of field is a bit technical, and if you're interested in physics, you may enjoy studying it more deeply. However, for most photographers, a general understanding of this concept is sufficient to execute it well in your images.

The depth of an image is the distance between the objects closest to your camera and the objects farthest from your camera. If you're photographing a person standing near the camera and there is a mountain range in the distance, you can understand that full distance as depth within the image.

However, depth of field refers to something more specific than this. Depth of field is the distance or depth that is *acceptably sharp* in the entire image. In other words, it's the depth you're able to capture that is reasonably in focus.

As you know, your camera can only focus with precision on a single object at a time, but levels of focus range from precise focus to total blur. You might deem parts of an image to be acceptably sharp when you can clearly see most of the details even if they aren't fully in focus.

An image with a person in the foreground and a mountain range far in the background probably has a narrow depth of field. This means that there is only a small range of distance within the photo that is acceptably sharp, likely the distance right around the person you're photographing.

However, if you take a photo of a person standing in the foreground and a cluster of trees behind them, you might end up with a photo that has much larger depth of field. As the photographer, you can choose whether you want to prioritize a narrow depth of field that focuses only one subject and leaves everything else blurry or a larger depth of field that also keeps other objects further back in the image in a reasonable amount of focus.

Depth of field is primarily adjusted using your aperture. Large apertures produce narrow depths of field, while small apertures produce larger depths of field. The other factor that contributes to depth of field is the distance between your camera and its subject. If you are close when taking your photograph, the resulting image will have a narrow depth of field. Your camera cannot effectively focus on something very close while also maintaining the clarity of objects in the background. When you are positioned further from your subject, you have more flexibility to incorporate a larger depth of field.

# [6]
# MASTERING WHITE BALANCE

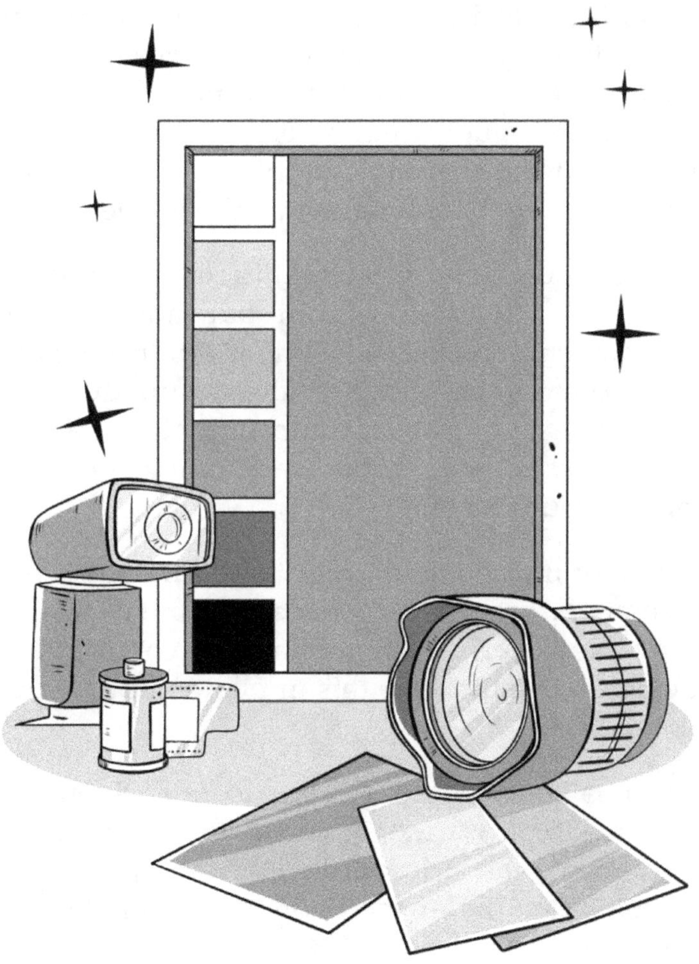

This guide has discussed some of the differences between light sources and light quality, and their importance to effective photography. You know that there are differences in the brightness of light at different times of day and that you need to compensate for this effectively when taking a photo. You also are now familiar with the concept of the "golden hour," renowned by photographers and artists for its warm, golden tones that appear beautifully when captured in images.

The quality of light during the golden hour helps to illustrate the idea of light's different tones and colors. For example, you know from everyday life that the light of the noon sun makes things look different than a fluorescent light in a department store. You may also have noticed that taking a photo with or without flash results in a different tone of light within the image.

Different sources of light produce different temperatures. This refers not to their actual temperature but rather to the sense of coolness or warmth in the quality of light produced. For example, candlelight produces an exceptionally warm quality of light, while cloudy skies tend to result in cool tones. In a photograph, these light sources will create an orange or blue tone, respectively, in your image.

Being mindful of the source of light that illuminates your photo, and its temperature is a crucial element of successful photography. However, you cannot always control the source of light that exists. To control for this in photography, you will rely on white balance.

White balance is your camera's ability to balance out the light in an image by making it warmer or cooler. Objects that may appear orange in an image taken in candlelight can appear more white (closer to their color under the noon sun) after they have been white balanced.

# AUTO WHITE BALANCE

Most cameras will automatically handle white balance in an image, subtly adjusting the colors of the image to appear more natural and less influenced by the light source. Auto white balance works by identifying the brightest part of your frame as the *white point* and then adjusting the colors in the image in relation to that area. It tends to work best outside in natural light. Indoor or artificial light is likely to have a more pronounced color tone besides pure white.

Auto white balance is convenient and allows photographs to be taken quickly, but the results aren't always ideal, especially when indoors. You may notice that your images appear more orange or blue than their natural appearance. If that's the case, you'll want to switch to using your camera's white balance presets or a custom/manual white-balance setting to better control the temperature of the light.

# PRESETS

White-balance presets are the options that your camera offers you for adjusting the color tone and white balance in an image. These might be settings such as *sun, cloudy, shade, tungsten, flash,* or *fluorescent,* which describe the type of lighting tone you aim to capture in an image.

Experiment with these settings by taking the same photo multiple times, once with each of the white-balance presets your camera provides. You'll notice the differences in color tone between these variations on the same image right away. Each will cast the photo in a slightly different light, some of which appear more natural than others to your eye.

# CUSTOM WHITE BALANCE

In addition to several white-balance preset options, your camera likely allows you to adjust your white balance manually to create a custom setting.

White balance is measured in degrees Kelvin, which refer to the warmth or coolness of the color tone produced. Lower numbers (e.g., 1,000 K) refer to the warmest tones, while higher numbers (e.g., 10,000 K) produce the coolest tones. Golden-hour light is around 3,000 K to 4,000 K, while a very overcast sky measures around 9,000 K to 10,000 K.

With a working knowledge of these ranges, you can create custom white-balance settings for the images you plan to take. For example, if an image comes out slightly too blue for your liking, you can adjust the white balance down. This will balance out the blue with more orange tones and create a more natural-looking image.

Most cameras provide a button that allows you to shift easily between white-balance presets, including custom or manual. You may also have to go into your camera's options menu to make these adjustments.

# USING GRAY CARDS

A white-balance card, also referred to as a gray card or an 18-percent gray card, is a tool you can use to precisely identify the optimal white balance for your image. The gray card is a physical card that you can purchase from a photography supplier or another store that you should carry with you alongside your other photography tools to any photo shoot.

To use this card, hold it up in front of the camera, allowing the camera to analyze it. Some cameras require that you take a picture of the gray card, while others analyze the card while it's in the viewfinder without requiring you to take a photo.

During this process, the camera is actually reading the temperature of light reflected from the card. It then uses that information to determine the optimal white balance for a photograph in your exact lighting environment. Each time you change the light slightly in the setting or move to a new angle or environment, you need to allow your camera to reanalyze the gray card so that it can readjust its white balance accordingly.

# [7]
# COMPOSITION TECHNIQUES

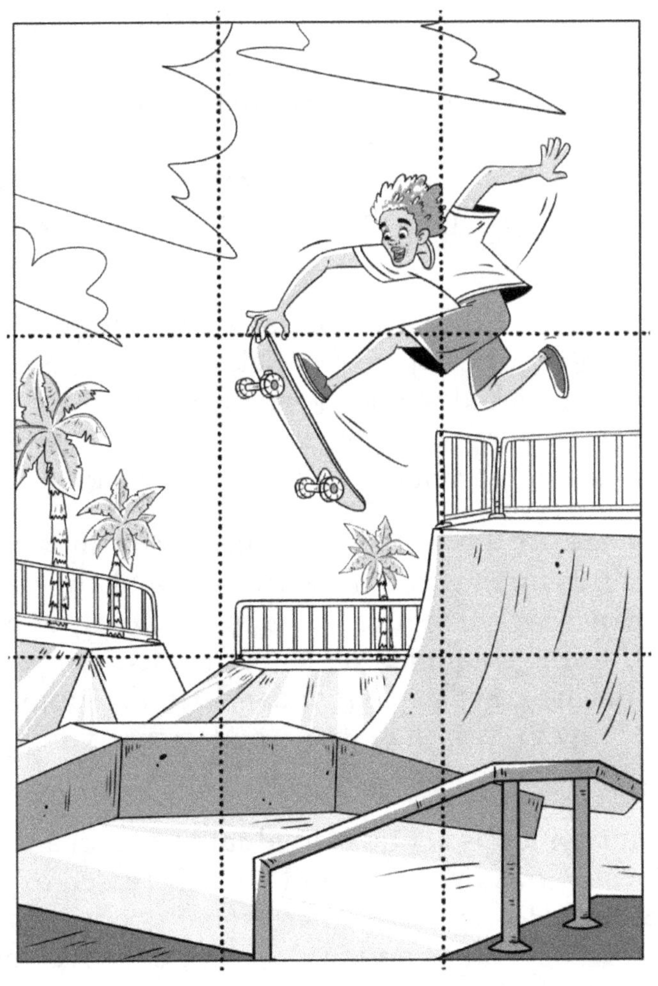

Composition is an exciting element of photography, one that allows any photographer's unique artistic vision and style to come through. We talked about composition in a basic way at the very start of this book as you began to understand the importance of what goes into an effective photograph. Now, with a greater understanding of lighting, shadow, focus, and white balance, you can approach composition from a more sophisticated point of view.

For example, you may take a photo that includes four cows, three trees, a red barn, and a distant lake. The arrangement of these items relative to one another within the frame of your picture is its composition. Are the cows in the foreground and to the left? Are the trees in the center of the image and the lake in the background to the right? Where is the red barn relative to the other objects?

Photographers know that it's not just what they photograph but how they arrange those objects that helps create a good picture. A good composition guides the viewer's eye through the image, implying relationships between the objects in the picture and articulating the photographer's intention for the photo.

If the cows are in the foreground and everything else in the background, this implies you meant to take a picture primarily of the cows. However, if the trees are in the foreground and the cows are off to the side, then perhaps the picture is primarily of the trees with the cows as a secondary detail. Composition and focus help convey these intentions and create variety, interest, and uniqueness among your images.

Much of composition is about individual intention and style, and you will develop this over time and with increased experience as a photographer. However, there are some good rules of thumb that will help you understand and master effective composition in your photos. Some of these include symmetrical and asymmetrical balance, framing, filling the frame, and watching the horizon.

# SIMPLICITY

The idea of simplicity is the same as the concept of minimalism in photography. Essentially, less is more. Simplicity in photography refers to taking photos that aren't overly complex or full of distracting details. You can create simplicity in your images by zooming in on a particular detail or focusing on a single subject and minimizing other distracting elements in the background.

For a straightforward example, imagine that you plan to take a photo of red tulips in a vase. If you place that vase of tulips in a room decorated with a vibrant, colorful wallpaper, the resulting image is going to be busy, complicated, and full of elements that catch the eye. In contrast, if you place that vase of tulips in front of a plain white wall, the resulting image will be simple and minimal.

Isolating your subject, seeking out empty backgrounds, and avoiding complex patterns are all ways to achieve simplicity or minimalism in your photos. Using a narrow depth of field or zooming in close with a macro lens are technical strategies to help you achieve this visual effect.

The preference for simplicity of composition is just that: a preference. There's no rule stating that images must be simple or minimalist, though this aesthetic is currently a popular one. You may decide that your preference is for complicated, maximalist photography if that better captures the feeling or meaning you want to convey in your images. Even if this is the case, mastering simplicity of composition is essential to diversify your photography skill set and create images that are likely to have broad appeal.

# RULE OF ODDS

The rule of odds is simple to understand yet may be unexpected. This rule states that when your photo will contain a group of subjects, using an odd number of subjects rather than an even number will result in a more interesting and appealing composition. If you're taking a photo of a grouping of apples on a table, make it three or five apples rather than two or four.

The reason for this rule of odds has nothing to do with the technical elements of your camera and everything to do with the way the human brain interprets images. When a grouping contains an even number of objects, let's say four, the brain automatically tends to group those objects into even pairs. The brain will perceive two groups of two rather than a single cohesive group of four. This trend toward symmetry and even grouping can result in images that feel somewhat dull, predictable, or overly organized.

In contrast, with an odd grouping, the brain cannot create those tidy symmetrical groups. It's left with a pattern that feels a bit more unusual and harder to organize, and that creates a more interesting and engaging image to view.

When organizing your odd-numbered groupings, you can choose the composition that best captures your intentions for the photo. For example, arranging three objects to fill your frame ensures that all three will be perceived as equally important in the image. Meanwhile, if you place one object clearly in the center of the frame and the others off to the side, then the one in the center becomes the focal point and the others are perceived as less important.

The rule of odds works in concert with the rule of thirds to provide interesting, meaningful photographic compositions.

# CENTERING THE SUBJECT

The concept of centering a subject has come up repeatedly throughout the sections on composition thus far. The decision to center—or not center—subjects is important when considering the rule of thirds, leading lines, symmetry, and framing.

There's no rule that says a subject must be centered within the photo frame, and you may often find that you prefer the subject off to the side. Alternatively, maybe the scene that you want to photograph doesn't allow you to control every detail of what's centered and what isn't; this creates lifelike, dynamic photography.

When considering whether or not to center your subject, here's one question to ask yourself: What is the best way to include everything important in this image? Sometimes, in order to include all the important elements, you'll need to position the subject in a strategic place within the frame. While the subject may or may not be centered, the priority is including everything you want in the photo.

You may decide whether or not to center your subject based on your preferences regarding symmetry. If you're taking a photo that has only one subject and you want your resulting image to be symmetrical, then it's essential to center the subject within the frame.

Depending on the type of focus you're using in an image, you may also rely upon a centered subject to achieve clarity. For example, if you want to zoom in close on a person's face or any other single object, your camera may focus best when its subject of focus is in the center of the frame.

# NEGATIVE SPACE

Negative space in an image can also be understood as "empty" space. The subject or subjects of your image are referred to as the *positive space*, and negative space stands in contrast to those. Picture an image of a full moon hanging in a dark, starless sky. The moon is the subject (positive space), and the darkness around it is the empty, or negative, space. Negative space is related to the concept of simplicity. It draws attention to the main subject by ensuring that the eye isn't distracted by other things.

Sometimes, negative space truly appears empty, as in the night sky example above. However, it doesn't always have to be truly empty or blank. A sense of negative space can be achieved by many compositions that ensure the surrounding or background areas of an image aren't distracting. Strategies for ensuring your backgrounds aren't distracting include using monochromatic color schemes, creating simple and symmetrical compositions, and prioritizing even textures.

For example, if you take a photograph of a flower against a background of grass, that grass serves as negative space as long as it's relatively monochromatic and evenly textured. If the grass is broken up by other small flowers, or if some of the grass is long and yellow-green while other sections are densely matted with dark-green clover, this might not provide a sense of negative space in the image. Negative space creates simplicity and facilitates clear focus, making it an important compositional strategy when you want to strongly emphasize your main subject.

# [8]
# UNDERSTANDING LENSES

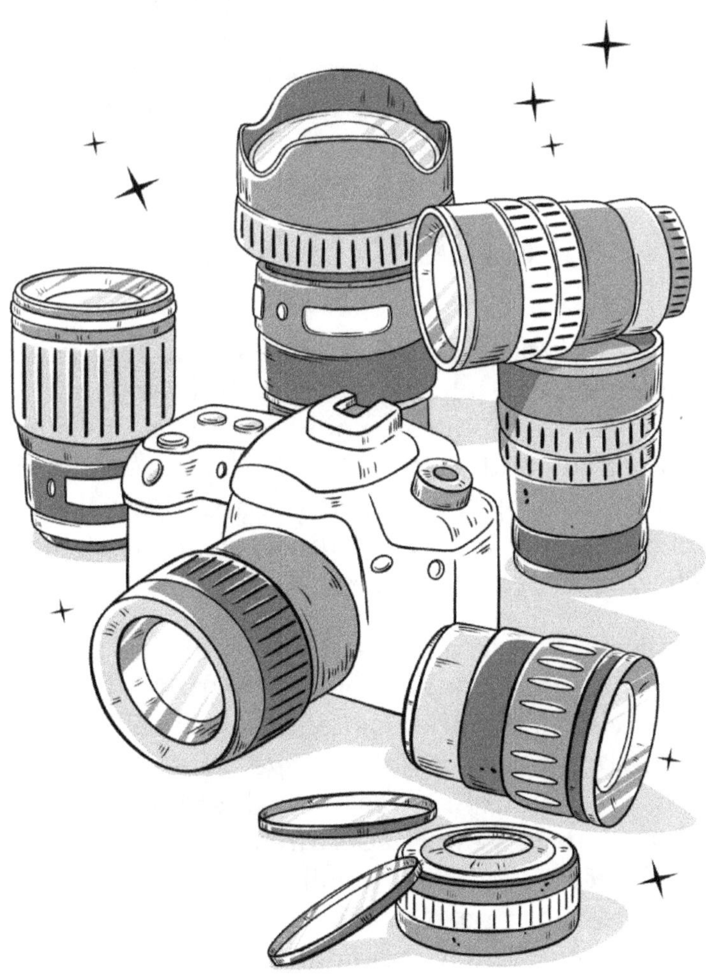

The lens is a crucial element of a camera without which it would only be possible to take pictures of pure white light. Camera lenses are made up of curved glass plates. They can be either convex or concave, and these glass plates work together to focus the light in your image.

When you look through the viewfinder, you see an image in front of your camera. The lens functions by focusing light from what you see through the viewfinder onto a tiny spot to produce the photographic image. Traditionally, it focused on film, but digital cameras now have digital sensors. This function is the core of photography, and as a result, the quality of your lens determines the quality of your photo.

# CHOOSING A LENS

There are several types of camera lenses including prime, zoom, macro, wide angle, and telephoto. With all these options, it can be difficult for a photographer to know which one to buy for their camera. It's worth conducting some in-depth research into your camera and its lens options when making these decisions. The key factors to consider are maximum aperture, cost, size, weight, compatibility, and special features.

Earlier in this book, we discussed apertures, as measured in f-stops. You know that the size of the aperture determines how much light will enter the camera, specifically the lens, to determine the brightness of your image. When you're looking at lenses to use on your camera, you'll see that each lists its maximum aperture. Wider apertures are best for low-light situations, but lenses with especially wide apertures often cost more than those with narrow apertures. Knowing the types of environments you plan to photograph in, and especially the amount and type of light to expect in those environments, will help guide you toward a lens that suits your purpose.

When considering cost, keep in mind that lenses tend to be expensive. If budget is a concern, you may want to opt for a middle-length zoom lens, which provides a range of functionality for a reasonable price. Size and weight also matter when choosing the lenses that are right for you. Some lenses can weigh far more than your camera itself, making them difficult to use when you need to be mobile during a photography session. If you intend to move around or travel with your lens, or if you expect you'll be carrying it long distances to reach a photo-shoot location, you may want to opt for a compact lens. However, if you know you'll need to capture high-quality photos from a long distance away, then a heavier telephoto lens may be your best choice.

Compatibility is an obvious feature to consider before purchasing a lens to accompany your camera. Not all lenses are compatible with all camera brands, so do your research ahead of time to determine which lens will work for you.

Finally, different lenses may offer unique features. You'll need to decide whether any of these bells and whistles are important to your work and photographic goals so that you can prioritize lenses that offer exactly what you need.

# FOCAL LENGTHS

Before diving deeper into the types of camera lenses available, it's necessary to have a basic understanding of focal lengths. Focal length controls the angle of view, which refers to how much of a scene will be captured in your image. Lens focal length also determines the magnification of an image, meaning how large the individual elements in the frame will appear.

Most new cameras offer a range of focal lengths that you can control. Each of these focal lengths provides a different angle of view and magnification in your photo. In general, a longer focal length (i.e., 100 mm or more) results in a narrower angle of view and higher magnification. In contrast, a shorter focal length (i.e.,

35 mm or less) creates an image with a wider angle of view and lower magnification.

Interestingly, the human eye has a focal length of 17 mm to 24 mm depending on the individual. The wide range of focal lengths available with camera lenses is a testament to the camera's ability to expand upon our relatively limited human optical functionality.

For many standard lenses, the typical focal length is 35 mm and 60 mm. These standard lenses (and focal lengths) work well across many situations including portraits and nature photography. By swapping out lenses, such as a telephoto lens or a wide-angle lens, you will access new ranges of focal lengths.

Choosing a long focal length lens (e.g., 135 mm or 200 mm) helps to create clarity and texture in distant backgrounds, while wide focal length lenses (e.g., 16mm or 24mm) help to keep an entire scene in focus.

# PRIME VS. ZOOM & OTHER TYPES OF LENSES

There are two fundamental categories of lenses: prime and zoom lenses. All other types and features of lenses fit into one of these overarching categories.

Prime lenses have a fixed focal length. This makes them fast, lightweight, and easy to use—perfect when you need to pack your camera equipment for travel. However, this fixed focal length makes prime lenses less adaptable to your needs.

If you want greater choice and control over focal length, you may want to use zoom lenses. Zoom lenses use a series of lenses to allow different focal lengths depending on your preferences. They are thus more flexible than prime lenses but not as quick to use. They also tend to be heavier and bulker than prime lenses overall.

Within prime and zoom lenses, you'll find there are a variety of lens types to choose from. For example, macro lenses are used to take very close-up, highly detailed, frame-filling photographs of a specific subject, making this a popular choice for nature photography. In contrast, telephoto lenses allow you to take a clear, high-quality image of a subject that is far away and can be useful for birdwatching or sports photography. Wide-angle lenses fit a very large area into the frame and are useful for landscapes. A fisheye lens builds upon a wide-angle lens to provide you with an extremely wide angle, capturing up to a 180-degree radius around the lens opening. This type of extreme angle can be useful but also results in distortion, which is important when considering the optimal camera lens for your use.

# LENS DISTORTION

Lens distortion is a very common issue in photography. While some photographers may intentionally seek distortion to capture a particular effect, many photographers see distortion as a problem. For this reason, it's important to learn how to control and prevent it as desired.

Lens distortion refers to elements of a photograph looking differently from how they appear in real life. You may be familiar with funhouse or carnival mirrors that distort the image you see when looking into them. For example, you could stand in front of a mirror that makes you look much taller or shorter, wider or narrower. This is distortion, and the effects created by those mirrors are the same effects that can appear in a distorted photo.

You may remember reading about leading lines earlier in this book. In effect, distortion is when those lines appear curved, and that curve then distorts all the elements within a photo. Perceiving this distortion in an image can be disorienting and unpleasant for the viewer, and it can detract from the reality of the resulting image.

There are three basic types of lens distortion: barrel, pincushion, and waveform. Different types of distortions are commonly associated with different lenses.

- Barrel distortion often results from a lens at full zoom.
- Pincushion distortion is most common with telephoto lenses.
- Waveform distortion results from wide-angle lenses in zoom mode.

Experiment carefully with the lens or lenses you use to find the balance between view angle, clarity, and precision in your images.

# [9]
# THE ART OF POSING

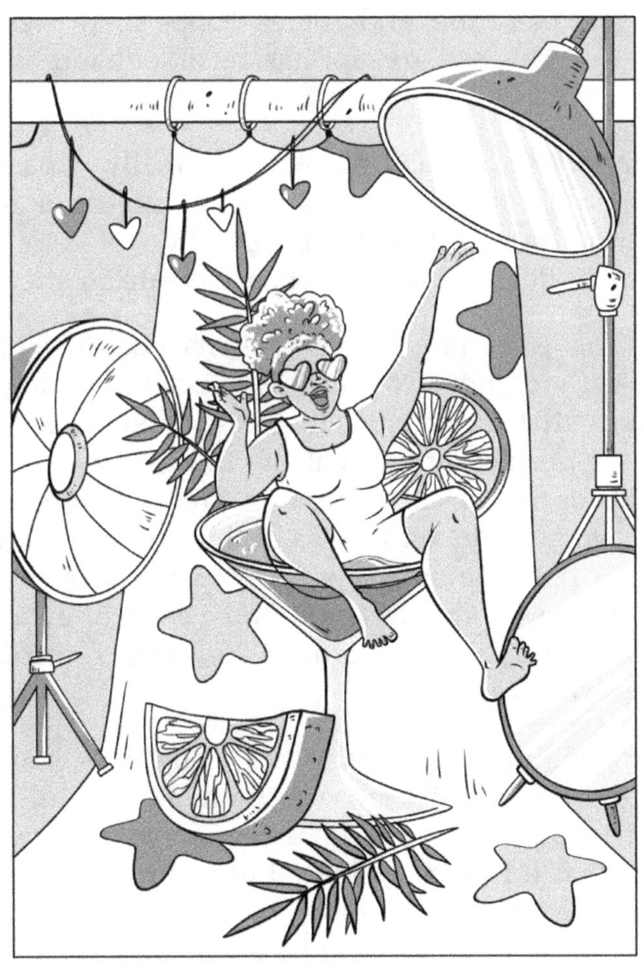

Posing refers to the positioning of a subject, especially a human subject, within a photo. A pose is created with intention, perhaps to generate interest, flatter the subject, or communicate emotion to the viewer. For example, a subject with their arms raised overhead may communicate triumph, while another subject with a hand scratching their chin may show thoughtfulness or indecision.

Poses are created through all kinds of movement and positioning, including rotation, tilting, and angles. Props such as clothing and accessories can be used to emphasize or enhance a particular pose.

Posing is important in photography as it really is part of the art itself. You may be lucky to work with a subject or model who knows how to pose effectively, but regardless of your subject, it's the responsibility of the photographer to create an effective pose.

We often think of posing in terms of its potential to flatter or make a subject look good. Most people prefer looking at images of themselves that emphasize the traits they're proud of and perhaps de-emphasize or conceal the things they don't favor as much. While each subject is unique and will prefer different poses, there are some general rules of thumb to create a flattering photograph. Angle the subject's chin up to make the neck and jawline visible, angle the subject's body slightly away from the camera, and avoid direct overhead lighting that might create unflattering shadows.

Beyond these simple rules and other techniques you'll pick up over time, the impact of a pose is both more subtle and more powerful than simple flattery. Part of what makes posing so important is that it has the potential to communicate so strongly with the viewer. You may have heard people say that most communication is nonverbal. In other words, humans do most of their communication through body language. The brain can easily interpret many gestures, expressions, and other forms of body language in order to find meaning from another person.

In fact, body language may be generally more trusted, and perceived to be more truthful, than the spoken or written word. Photography has the power to capture that body language effectively and with great impact, so it's important to harness the potential of a pose and use it to your intended effect.

# PORTRAITURE

Posing is important in formal portraiture. Unlike in candid shots, you'll likely have the time and ability to carefully design or direct a pose when taking a portrait, making it vital to pose your subject well.

One common mistake in posing a subject for a portrait is to simply direct them to smile ("say cheese!"). While people generally enjoy viewing images of people smiling, a false smile for the sake of a photograph isn't likely to convey happiness. At its worst, it might convey awkwardness and discomfort if their smile felt forced. A true smile engages the entire face and especially the eyes. A person viewing a photo will be able to tell easily whether a subject's smile was real or forced, so it's the job of photographer to elicit authentic smiles for portraits.

Rather than simply telling a subject to smile, build rapport and ensure the subject is comfortable with you and the plans for the photograph. Next, get them talking about something that makes them happy. Share your own happy story or even crack a joke. Your goal is to prompt a genuine smile that conveys the happiness of an authentic moment. Regardless of the position of the rest of the subject's body, capturing that true smile will be an important element of the final portrait.

Another important element to consider is the angle of the subject's body to the camera. Photographing someone straight on conveys a sense of their confidence, comfort, and power. However, it can also cause the image to feel dull or predictable if it's entirely symmetrical and lacks other elements of interest.

Photographing from the side or at an angle can reduce that implication of confidence or even suggest vulnerability in some cases.

Experiment with angling a body away from the camera but keeping the face straight on, or vice versa. These combinations can provide a good balance of interest and confidence in a photograph, and you can adjust each element of the pose to find a position that best reflects the personality of your subject.

# CANDID SHOTS

Unlike formal portraiture, in which the frame is carefully planned and controlled, candid shots are taken without a lot of advanced planning. Candid shots aim to capture a real-life moment in time, perhaps a child's first steps or a grandparent blowing out candles on a milestone birthday cake. You won't have time to carefully pose and orchestrate these images; sometimes, you may not even know they're about to happen. Regardless of whether you can provide some posing instructions to your subjects or not, the following tips can help ensure your candid photos look natural.

First, a moderate amount of motion is your ally in candid photography. Rather than taking a photo of a group of people standing together, perhaps bunched awkwardly or not sure how to interact with one another, try taking the photo of the group while they're walking toward or away from you. When people are in motion, their body language and positioning is likely to be more natural, and these photos can feel truer to life than photos that are unnaturally static. Likewise, any small or moderate movement, like taking off sunglasses, adjusting a hat, or kicking a pebble along the sidewalk can create that sense of authentic movement and relaxation.

Adding a prop, or prioritizing shots that incorporate a prop, can also be a great technique for creating fun and candid photos. For example, you can have your subject hold something and interact with it, like looking at a delicious ice cream cone they're about to eat or handing you a flower.

Sitting down can be another good option to create a sense of relaxation. Likewise, having a subject cross one arm, lean against a wall, or even jump into the air can create interest and infuse a sense of life into candid shots.

# GROUP PHOTOGRAPHY

Group photography can refer to either formal, posed portraiture or unplanned candid shots. An example of formal group portraiture may be an annual photo taken at a family reunion or a group of children posed together on their first day of school. The same ideas described above for individual portraiture still apply here. Encourage your subjects to feel comfortable and work to achieve authentic smiles. You may need to angle your subjects to fit them all in the frame, though this is also a good time to try out wider-angle lenses if you're able to control for distortion.

When taking candid group photos — perhaps a group of friends at the beach during a vacation — keep these ideas in mind to make sure your photos look natural rather than awkward. Encourage the group to interact with each other, with props, or with their environment. Try having them walk or move around together so that you can capture those moments of natural movement in the image rather than keeping things stiff or controlled.

When working with a group, especially in a candid setting, you'll need to be mindful of effective composition. All the compositional techniques discussed so far are important when photographing multi-subject images; symmetry, the rule of thirds, effective framing, and the use of negative space will all come into play. For example, consider whether you want one person to stand out as the primary focus or whether everyone should be balanced equally across the frame.

Since you can't always control for all these factors when taking candid shots, you may find that you need to take more photos in these situations. One or two carefully planned shots may be enough to capture a great portrait. However, in a candid photo shoot, assume you'll take many more to get those perfect images.

# [10]
# POST-PROCESSING ESSENTIALS

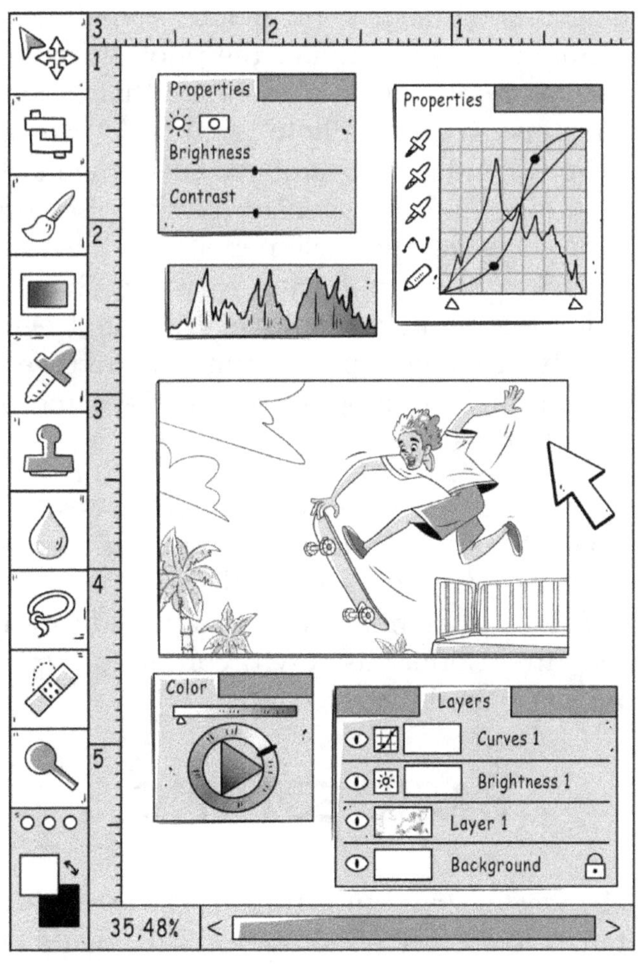

So far, everything in this book has been related to the time before a photo is taken (e.g., choosing a lens or posing subjects) and the moment the image is captured (e.g., choosing aperture and shutter speed). While these are crucial elements of photography, a photographer's job isn't done as soon as the image is created. The work that continues afterward to finalize the image before distribution is known as *post-processing* or *photo editing*.

Post-processing allows the photographer to take unrefined or imperfect images and make them better. Sometimes, this is as simple as cropping out a portion of the photo that wasn't meant to be included or removing a bumblebee that landed on your subject's head just as the photo snapped. However, post-processing also includes substantive adjustments for artistic purposes, often involving the transformation of colors, lighting, focus, and other photographic elements to achieve a particular visual effect. Through photo editing, you can sharpen a photo, change its color temperature, remove unwanted elements, and much more. Advanced post-processing can involve combining elements from multiple photographs into the same image (e.g., adding a person to the scene).

These days, post-processing most often takes place on a computer, tablet, or other device. There are numerous apps and software programs designed specifically for photo editing that offer a combination of standard and unique editing tools. Your camera brand may offer its own compatible photo-editing software, which is a good place to start.

## BASIC EDITING

The first and most basic editing function, which photographers use quite often, is to correct a photograph's exposure by adjusting the overall brightness of the image. You may need to brighten an image that came out too dark for clarity or reduce the brightness of an overexposed image. If needed, refer to the section on reading the histogram, which provides an overview of how to measure exposure in your image. Photo-editing software will provide easy functionality for you to adjust the exposure until you achieve the balanced histogram that you desire.

Another basic editing function is to adjust your photo's saturation. Saturation refers to the intensity of colors in an image. By increasing saturation, you can make the colors in an image appear more vibrant, giving your image an extra boost of energy. Alternatively, you can reduce saturation if you desire a result that looks slightly more muted.

Another basic editing technique you're likely to use is sharpening. Sharpening makes the edges within a photo clearer. While sharpening can't be used to fix a photo that's completely blurry, it can help create more focus around edges that might have been blurred in the original photograph. Many, or even most, photos can benefit from some subtle sharpening. However, it's important to be careful not to significantly sharpen faces or other human features that will quickly look unnatural when they've been adjusted.

With basic editing techniques, the goal is to create a slightly improved image that still looks authentic. Viewers should not be able to point out where you've adjusted an image, as the edits typically serve to make it look more natural.

# ADVANCED EDITING TECHNIQUES

Advanced post-processing goes beyond enhancing the clarity and quality of natural images. More advanced editing usually aims to take the photo beyond the boundaries of what's realistic into either an idealized photo or the realm of imagination.

For example, many of us are aware that magazine images are heavily edited to create an idealized result that no longer looks quite like the original human subject. In this advanced editing, the size and shape of photographic elements can be modified alongside adjustments to lighting, shadow, texture, and other features to create what is essentially a whole new image. In some cases, the final photograph showcases a person who is unrecognizable from their actual appearance.

Instead of editing for an idealized result, many photographers use advanced post-processing to realize an imaginative artistic vision that wouldn't be possible to photograph. For example, advanced editing can be used to make it appear that a human subject has wings and is flying through the clouds or that a pair of cats have dressed up in tuxedos for a fancy dinner. Advanced photo editing provides truly unlimited potential to create images that reflect your imagination.

Some of this more advanced editing represents a higher level of the basic editing skills described above, such as adjusting color tone and shadow. However, new techniques are possible as well once you develop past the basics.

One of these is the use of layering in photo editing, which refers to layering elements from one photo on top of another. In this process, imagine that the photo on top is made of glass. Even when it's on top of another, the photo on the bottom is still visible "through" the image that covers it. In this way, two photos can appear to blend into one.

Image masking, or using masks, is another advanced editing technique. This technique involves isolating one element in a photo from the rest of the image. For example, you may have taken a picture of a dog sitting in front of a large flowering shrub. Through image masking, you could isolate the dog and essentially erase, or mask, that shrub in pure white. This leaves you with just the dog against an empty background, perfect for then layering with another image.

There are innumerable, increasingly advanced techniques for photo editing available to those with the patience and skill to master them. New options are developed all the time. By starting with the basics and then expanding into layering and masking, you'll have the necessary foundation to dive deeper into the most advanced types of photographic post-processing.

# WORKFLOW OPTIMIZATION

In photography, the full process of capturing, editing, processing, and finalizing digital images is referred to as your *workflow*. As you gain experience as a photographer over time, you'll want to find ways to optimize this workflow by making it as streamlined, standardized, and efficient as possible.

In your day-to-day life, you may already have your own personal systems for staying organized—perhaps using shared calendars, writing detailed to-do lists, or leveraging productivity and note-taking apps. Likewise, as a photographer, you will develop a system for keeping your images and processes organized.

Some of these are simple tips that may already be familiar to you. For example, when downloading digital images to your computer for editing, develop an organized folder system that allows you to quickly store, find, and sort all your images.

Another good tip is to be intentional about how much time you spend editing images. Editing is a focused, detailed process that requires all your attention, and it can be easy to lose track of time while doing it. When that happens, your attention to detail can begin to flag as your energy wanes, and you won't be able to produce optimal results. For that reason, it's a good idea to decide how much time is reasonable for you to spend editing per day and set a timer to keep yourself on track. If you plan to work for more than an hour at a time, set timers to remind yourself to take a break. Get up, walk around, drink water, and reset your energy and attention before diving back in.

Another good tip to keep in mind for optimizing your workflow is to build in a buffer day after you finish editing but before you export or share an image. Once you finish editing and save your image, you may be tempted to share it immediately. However, taking one more look at it the next day with fresh eyes can be helpful for catching any small issues.

# PRESETS AND FILTERS

Presets and filters are tools you can use to better optimize your workflow. Useful presets include automated settings for folders or automated export settings for image size and quality that match your most common needs.

Depending on the software you're using to edit your images, you may be able to set up lighting presets as well. These come in handy if you're editing batches of images from the same setting and the same lighting context. For example, if you took several images in a series of a child blowing out candles on a birthday cake, applying lighting presets to the full series at once will save you the time it would otherwise take to painstakingly make the same edits on each photo individually. To do this, edit one image from the series manually to find the ideal lighting, then apply those carefully selected settings as a preset to all the other photos.

Filters—typically either circular or square—are an essential part of many photographers' workflows. Filters attach to your camera's lens to have a particular impact on each photo. You may want to experiment with polarizing filters, which provide more saturated colors and greater contrast. You can also explore neutral density (ND) filters that decrease shutter speed and can be used to capture long-exposure images.

Filters can be made of either glass or resin. You may find that you have a favorite or that you tend to use both. Some argue that glass filters produce images with more clarity, though a benefit to resin filters is that they are hardier and less likely to break than their glass counterparts. However, resin filters are prone to scratching. Experiment with both to find the filters that work best for your typical photography style and photographic conditions.

Some types of filters serve to protect your camera itself, thereby allowing you to shoot in otherwise difficult conditions. For example, skylight filters prevent dust and moisture from accumulating on the lens and also protect it from scratching. UV filters protect film from intense UV light, which could otherwise cause images to appear hazy.

Incorporating the appropriate lens into your photo session optimizes your workflow by controlling for potential hazards or implementing specific effects in advance, reducing the editing time you need to spend later.

# [11]
# LANDSCAPE PHOTOGRAPHY TIPS

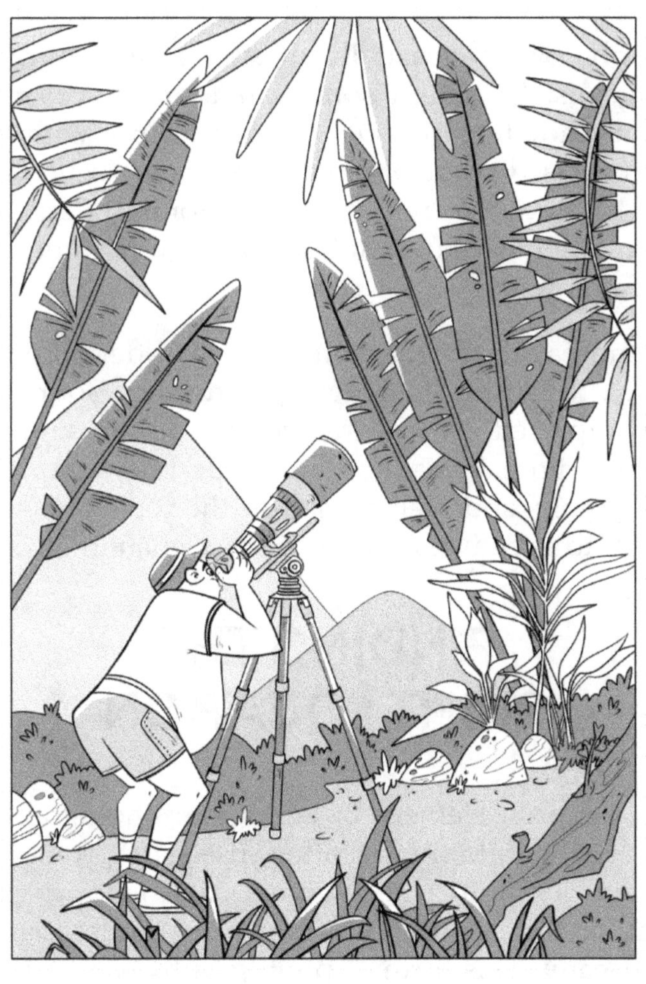

We have mentioned various types of photography, including portraiture, nature photography, and casual candid shots. One of the most dramatic areas of photography, which is both uniquely challenging and rewarding, is landscape photography. Landscape photography generally refers to images captured outdoors in natural light, showcasing natural features such as land, sky, and water. Landscape photography typically, though not exclusively, captures these elements at a distance rather than close up.

Landscape photography usually doesn't feature human activity in the image itself, though some landscape photography does capture man-made features such as architecture within its scope. For example, this type of photography could focus on urban or industrial landscapes, not only pastoral ones. Landscape photography often captures stationary subjects rather than those actively in motion.

Because landscape photography is, by definition, outdoor photography, it can be challenging to master. Your images will always be impacted by natural conditions of sunlight, wind, humidity, and more. An adept landscape photographer must be nimble, adaptable, and well versed in the tools and strategies at their disposal to effectively adjust to those changing conditions.

# FINDING THE RIGHT LOCATION

Location is a crucial element of landscape photography. In fact, this form of photography is often used to promote tourism, factoring heavily into the success of national parks like Yellowstone or the popularity of beautiful landscapes like those found in Tuscany. This form of photography can have enormous economic, behavioral, and cultural impacts. Landscape photography has the power to transport viewers from their own surroundings to other parts of the world, a true testament to the power of a compelling image.

There are many factors that go into choosing a location for landscape photography. Since this type of photography is so broad in definition—urban or rural, meant to inspire tourism or meant to inspire a sense of isolation—there are no set rules for how it should be done. Part of determining the optimal location for your own landscape photography will be clearly identifying your goals for your images.

Do you want to simply capture a beautiful vista? Or do you want to instill a sense of adventure or wonder in your viewers? Do you seek to capture the beauty of a place that might not be traditionally considered beautiful? Is your photography meant to motivate more people to visit a special spot? All these goals could inspire your landscape photography, and knowing what you set out to do is the first step.

You'll also need to carefully consider the weather and lighting conditions of your chosen landscape. As you've learned already through this guide, those conditions will determine your exposure settings, the lenses you might need to have on hand, and any editing considerations you can plan for in advance.

You should also consider whether the landscape you seek to capture is likely to be static or active. A forest or mountain shot at distant range will create a photo that appears static, while a shot of an ocean on a windy day taken at closer range will convey more movement. These factors determine your shutter speed and other settings necessary to capture the image you seek.

# CAPTURING DYNAMIC SKIES

You may have seen images before that capture luminous, dramatic, or unusual skies. These images tend to be memorable across wide and diverse audiences, and many photographers are inspired to try to capture them.

Capturing dynamic skies in your landscape photography can be a technical challenge. Daytime skies can be extremely bright even on a cloudy day, making the resulting images appear washed out. To avoid this, use smaller apertures and low ISO settings, and consider adding an ND filter. If you hope to capture natural movement in the skies, perhaps the northern lights or the motion of the clouds, you can do so with slow shutter speeds.

Polarizing filters can also be useful for capturing dramatic images of the skies. A polarizing filter helps reduce glare and deepen colors, making it a great tool to have at your disposal for landscape photography in general.

Don't underestimate the power of post-processing to enhance, sharpen, and refine your images. Adjusting white balance, clarity, saturation, contrast, and more can help perfect your images. Be careful not to overdo it; the result should still look natural. The goal of photo editing in this case is to better capture how the scene actually appeared to the human eye rather than creating something that goes beyond that to the supernatural.

## USING FILTERS

As mentioned above, polarizing and ND filters can be very useful in landscape photography. In addition to deepening colors, a polarizing filter reduces the appearance of reflections and glare off the water, making it very useful in damp outdoor conditions.

Neutral density filters reduce the total amount of light entering the lens, which can be very helpful when using slow shutter speeds in landscape photography. You may want to try a graduated neutral density (GND) filter as well for a more advanced approach.

A GND filter is divided between a darker part and a lighter part with a gradual transition between them. This is useful in practice because you can position the filter such that its darker part serves to darken the brightest area of the image in your frame (usually the sky), while the lighter part of the filter brightens up darker areas in the frame. In this way, a GND filter can balance exposure right at the outset, hopefully without either over- or under-exposing any part of your photo.

# INCORPORATING FOREGROUND INTEREST

While landscape photography typically aims to capture a large area at a distance, such as a  mountain range or miles of prairie, that doesn't mean the photographer can ignore what's happening in the foreground. In landscape photography, *foreground* refers to the bottom third of your composition.

The foreground of a landscape photo is important in part based on the rule of thirds. In order to achieve a balanced composition in your photo, you likely don't want part of it to be empty of interest. You can use the foreground strategically to frame the areas of interest in your photo or to ensure effective leading lines are incorporated to lead the viewer's eye where you want it to go. In landscape photography, this often means leading the eye from the foreground of the image to the middle distance or even to the background.

When selecting foreground interest, look for patterns, textures, bold colors, and natural leading lines. These tend to work best if they're natural elements of the landscape you're photographing, though they don't necessarily need to be. For example, you may take a picture of a field of flowers, using a roughly textured wooden bench in front of the field as your foreground interest.

Elements like tall flowers in your foreground can help direct the eye upward without distracting from the interesting middle distance and background. Graphic texture also provides terrific foreground interest even in the absence of a specific object. For example, if you are photographing the ocean, you may choose to highlight rough sand and shell piles in the foreground. These are naturally occurring elements within the landscape that provide visual texture at the bottom third of the image to balance the ocean and sky.

# [12]
# MASTERING THE ART OF MACRO

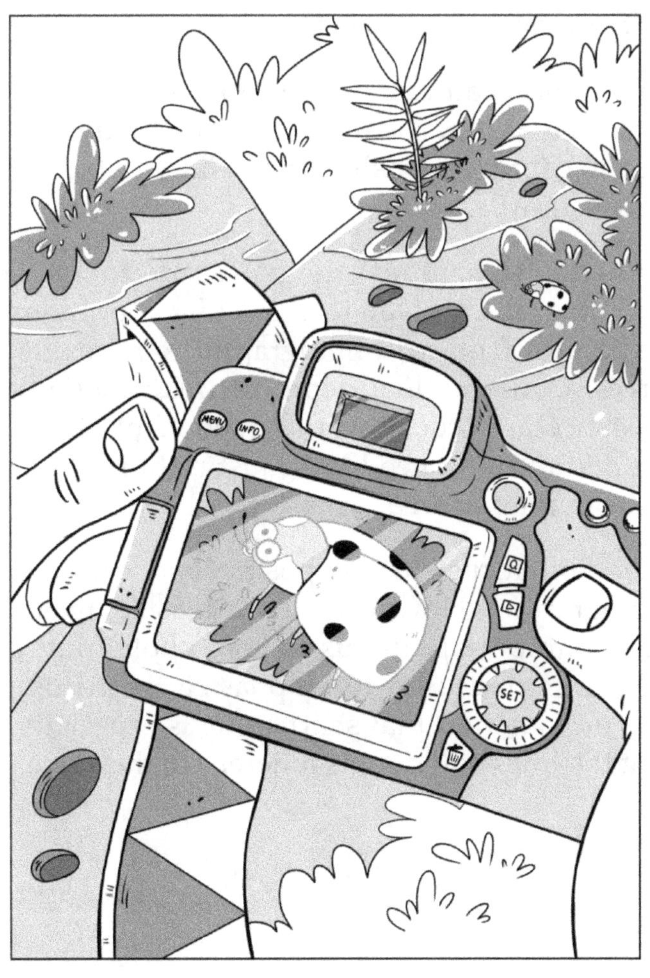

Landscape photography is often about photographing nature's biggest, epic wonders: the Rockies, the Grand Canyon, the Pacific Ocean. From that grand scale, we shift to macro photography, which allows you to capture tiny objects and details with focus and precision. This type of photography celebrates the beauty and grandeur inherent in even the smallest photographic subjects. It allows the viewer to appreciate levels of texture, hue, and detail that aren't always immediately visible to the naked eye. Macro photography results in images of objects that appear at or larger than their natural size.

Macro photography can be used to capture a precise image of a small object, such as a particularly charming ladybug. It can also be leveraged to capture a small part of a larger object, like a single petal on a large flower.

Just like specific techniques are necessary to maximize your landscape photography, given its particular conditions and goals, mastering the art of macro photography requires its own skills and resources. Concepts like depth of field, magnification, and working distance are crucial in this type of photography where the lighting and framing need to be just right in order to achieve optimal focus in a small area.

This chapter will focus on composing and capturing effective macro photography. However, that doesn't mean the post-processing is unimportant in this style of photography. Cropping and resizing are often used to emphasize the focus of a macro image, and you may find that sharpening is especially helpful for highlighting the lines and details inherent to this style.

# CHOOSING THE RIGHT EQUIPMENT

Your ability to capture a successful photo will depend to some extent upon the equipment you're using. Using a camera with particular features and capabilities will enable you to achieve more in macro photography, so you should focus on those characteristics when deciding which equipment to use.

Macro photography requires a high-resolution sensor, which is a built-in feature of some cameras. These sensors capture plenty of light and result in more detailed, less noisy images—essential for macro shots. Closely related to this is the idea of image quality. You'll need to choose a camera that reliably delivers color fidelity and optimal contrast in your photos, as well as one that you know how to work with to adapt quickly to diverse lighting contexts.

You will need to invest in a macro lens in order to seriously pursue macro photography. Macro lenses are those that have focal lengths between 90 mm and 105 mm, providing you with more working distance in your images. For those who enjoy experimentation, you can achieve macro images without a dedicated macro lens through strategies like reversing a wide or normal lens, using equipment like extension tubes or bellows, or adding a strong macro filter. There are pros and cons to each of these options. The cost savings is offset by a loss of other helpful features like auto-focus.

Additional items that are relevant to macro photography include flash diffusers, ring lights, and macro rails. The latter allow you to refine your focus much more precisely, making them well suited to magnified photography.

# DEPTH OF FIELD
# IN MACRO

Earlier in this book, the section on focusing techniques introduced you to the concept of depth of field. You may recall that depth of field is the distance or depth that's acceptably sharp in an image. It may be helpful to review that content before moving on, to ensure that you grasp the basics, as an understanding of depth of field is crucial to macro photography.

When you're taking an extreme close-up with macro photography, an insufficient depth of field may leave much of your subject blurry. For example, if you're photographing an interesting insect on a twig, you may decide to focus on its eye. If your depth of field is insufficient, then the eye may be in focus, but the rest of the insect's body may appear blurry. By optimizing your depth of field, you'll maintain clarity over a larger area of your subject.

Typically, depth of field is determined by aperture value, focal length, and your distance from your subject. However, in macro photography, depth of field is primarily determined by aperture value and magnification. Since macro photography magnifies the subject of the image, the depth of field is always going to be relatively shallow. The image is always covering a small area when measured, for example, in inches. Working within this large magnification and shallow depth of field, your challenge as the macro photographer is to still ensure clarity and sufficient focus across the important parts of your image.

One way to maximize your depth of field in macro photography is to angle your camera so that you are shooting across a relatively flat plain, or at least as flat as you can make it. For example, if you aim to take a macro photo of an inchworm, do it from the side so that your image will be along the relatively flat plane of the worm's body. By working with this flat plane, you can more easily achieve sharp focus over the full inchworm. This would be better compared to taking the photo head on, which would require you to try to focus on the worm's head without the rest of the body being a blur.

A more advanced technique for achieving macro focus is focus stacking. Focus stacking is using the layering technique in photo editing to layer images that have captured different depths of focus on the same object. By layering these levels of focus, you can come up with a composite image that appears to have an optimal depth of field.

# LIGHTING IN MACRO PHOTOGRAPHY

Macro photography often requires a very narrow aperture in order to obtain sufficient depth of field. As a result, it's essential to ensure there is adequate light in the scene to brighten the photo despite that narrow aperture.

The optimal lighting for macro photography is diffuse bright sunlight. This provides enough light without creating too much unnatural contrast, which may result from improperly balanced artificial light sources. If you are using artificial light, such as a flash or continuous indoor light, you will want to diffuse or filter it to soften the light and reduce any sense of harshness in the image.

One reason that lighting can be so challenging in macro photography is that you tend to be shooting photos with a very small distance between the camera lens and its subject. Thus, even if your setting is quite bright, there simply isn't much space for light to get in.

If you're confident that your subject will stay perfectly still, such as an inanimate object, then you have the option of using a tripod and slower shutter speed to capture your macro image. The slower shutter speed allows more light to enter, and the use of the tripod ensures that your camera will remain absolutely still while the shutter is open. This is essential to avoid blur in the image.

LED ring lights that attach directly to your camera's lens are a newer technology that can be extremely useful in macro photography. Since the light affixes to the lens itself, you can typically avoid the problem of shadows created by the camera, as well as the challenges that result from low subject distance.

# COMPOSING MACRO SHOTS

The goal of macro photography is typically to "wow" the viewer with a high-impact, high-detail image. A macro shot provides a close view on details that people can't otherwise see, so they tend to be bold, attention grabbing, and memorable. However, all this power in the image can be reduced or eliminated by poor composition. When you aim to capture a subject in detail, your photo must be composed precisely to do just that.

It goes without saying that a macro photograph must have a subject: one specific, easily identifiable subject that any viewer would name as the focus of the image. Macro photography is not the technique to use for groups of subjects or disparate objects. Rather, there must be a clear, single point of focus in the image that stands out to the viewer.

Based on the rule of thirds, an ideal placement for your subject in a macro photograph is one-third of the way into the frame. Thus, the ladybug or inchworm would be off center as you picture the rule-of-thirds gridlines that guide placement and composition.

Alternatively, you may choose to center your subject. In this case, it's most impactful to aim for symmetry in the photo. A macro symmetrical composition can fill your frame and will naturally draw in viewers who are predisposed to enjoy looking at symmetrical images. In general, filling the frame is an exciting technique available to you when practicing macro photography. However, if you choose not to fill the frame with your subject, then aim for a neutral and flat background so that your subject remains the clear, unambiguous focal point of the image.

# [13]
# UNDERSTANDING COLOR THEORY

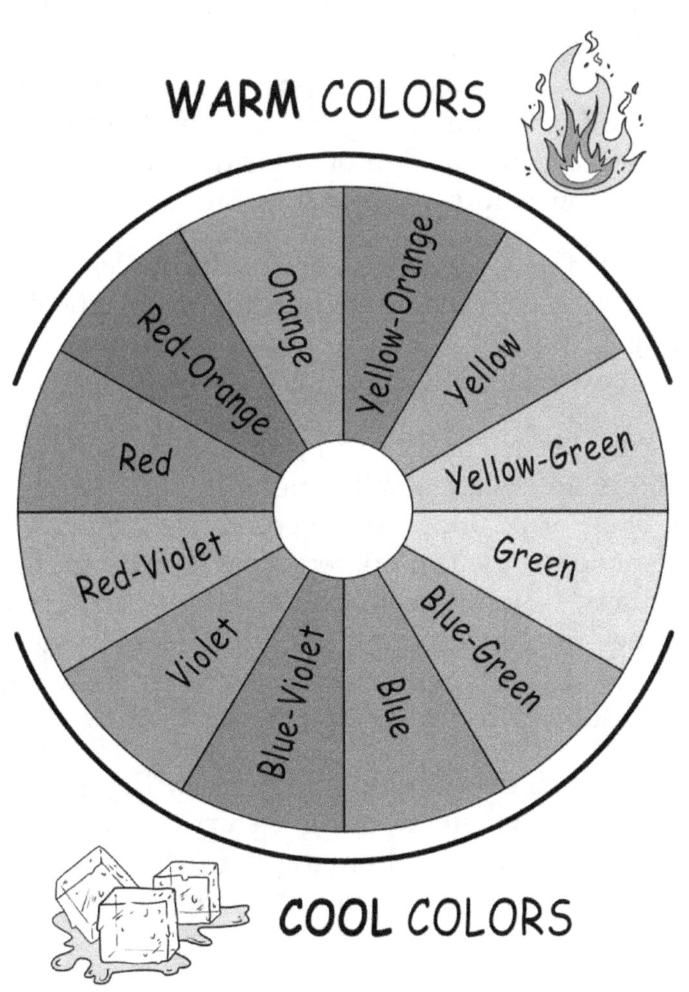

In its most general sense, color theory governs the way humans see, perceive, and use color. It is considered both a science and an art. It's essential to understand that color is perception. Each object reflects light in a unique combination of wavelengths. When these wavelengths reach our eyes, our eyes send a message to our brain telling it which color to perceive.

In elementary school, you likely learned about primary colors and the secondary colors you can create from combining different primaries. Red and blue make purple; blue and yellow make green, and so on. Tertiary colors such as red-violet or yellow-orange are made by combining primary and secondary colors. This is a very basic application of color theory, which enables us to understand how colors mix and how our eyes perceive them.

Color theory also includes ideas about color matching or contrast that you may already know based on the color wheel. The color wheel arranges primary, secondary, and tertiary colors around a wheel in rainbow order.

Through color theory, people can attain some insight into how different colors and color combinations impact people's feelings and behaviors. For example, some colors are known to enhance appetite or make people feel bolder; these are commonly used for selling products. Colors like soft blues and greens are known to inspire feelings of relaxation and are often used in spas. Color is important, and it has tangible impacts on our daily experiences both as individuals and as a society.

We use the basic tenets of color theory every day when deciding how to decorate or when choosing a shirt that looks good with the color of our pants. As a photographer, your understanding of color theory will need to go beyond this everyday usage.

# COLOR HARMONIES

Color harmonies are how we perceive the interactions between different colors. Color harmony is based on the color wheel and uses geographic relationships between colors' placements on that wheel to identify combinations perceived as harmonious.

Colors that are opposites on the color wheel, such as red and green, are sharply in contrast to one another and considered complementary colors. Their contrast creates a strong and memorable impact. They're good for a quick impression but potentially exhausting if overused.

Analogous colors are those near to each other on the color wheel, such as red and orange. These colors are perceived as similar and lacking stark contrast. In an analogous color scheme, one color usually comes across as dominant and the other comes across as the supporting color. These harmonies tend to be perceived as more soothing rather than jarring.

Triadic colors are those spaced at even intervals around the color wheel, such as red, yellow, and blue. When placed side by side, the combination is dynamic and cheerful, neither too contrasting nor too similar.

These are some of the most common schemes one may consider when arranging colors together in a space, outfit, brand, logo, or image. These different harmonies, in addition to the colors themselves, can influence people's thoughts, feelings, and behaviors. Thus, as a photographer, you want to be intentional and strategic about selecting and arranging colors within an image to create your desired effect. You may know instinctively that a mostly dark-colored photo will not be perceived as energetic and upbeat. Color theory and color harmonies are what explain that instinct scientifically so that you can put it to good use as an artist.

# USING COLOR TO CONVEY EMOTION

Specific colors both convey and inspire specific emotions. For example, blue is known to convey sadness, but it may inspire feelings of relaxation. Red can be used to convey anger but also show love. Color symbolism can be either scientifically based or culturally dependent. In the latter case, different colors mean different things to different cultures around the world. While some cultures wear black to symbolize mourning, other cultures use white for the same purpose. Thus, the import of these colors is not biologically ingrained but rather culturally defined.

When planning your photography, you need to bear in mind the science behind color theory and the known power of color harmonies to convey tone and mood. You also need to be informed of the cultural context of your target audience and any significance that audience may assign to particular colors or color combinations. While this may sound like a tall order, rest assured that many of these considerations will come naturally. After all, you are a product of your own culture, so you are already familiar with the significance of certain colors.

In general, colors on the warm side of the color wheel — red, orange, and yellow — evoke feelings of happiness, energy, and passion. These colors remind us of sunshine, lightning, and fire. Colors on the cool side of the color wheel — blue, green, purple — are thought to convey feelings of calm or even sadness. For many people, pink represents romance, while white signifies innocence. These associations are very strong in most people's minds, and therefore you should use them to your advantage when taking photos that you intend to convey a specific mood.

It's not uncommon for artists, including photographers, to have their own unique relationships with colors. You may have your own preferred palettes or color combinations that you find yourself calling on again and again simply because they're appealing to you. This is perfectly okay, as your images will represent your own perspective as an individual and an artist. However, it's worth being aware of how others may interpret elements in your photography, including how they may respond to certain color schemes.

# BALANCING COLOR IN A PHOTO

The most important color balance to consider in a photo is always going to be your white balance. However, through careful composition and post-processing, you can be strategic about balancing the intensities and contrasts of other colors in your images as well so that no single color unintentionally outweighs another.

When it comes to balancing colors from the perspective of psychological impact, the most important thing is ensuring that skin tones and other personal attributes are rendered with fidelity. If the grass looks a bit neon or the blue sky unrealistically sapphire, that may impact the aesthetic impact of the image, but it won't drastically change the appearance of human subjects.

# [14]
# STORYTELLING THROUGH PHOTOGRAPHY

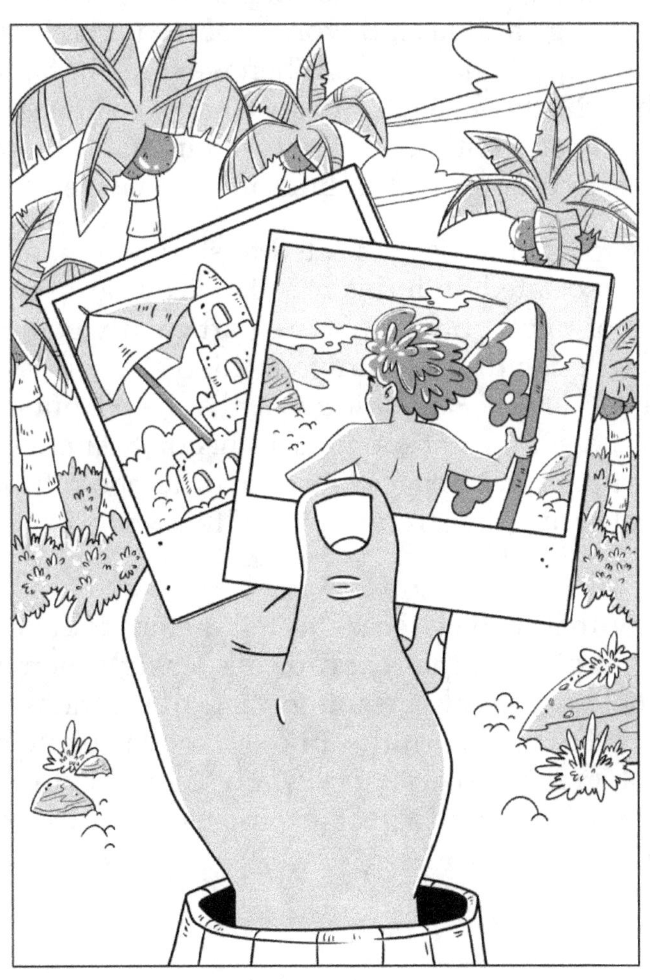

You have almost certainly heard the popular phrase, "A picture is worth a thousand words." Interestingly, this statement is used in several world languages, conveying a universal truth that can carry a great deal of meaning. Powerful images can convey a depth of emotion and sometimes seem to tell a broader story about a person, place, or moment in time just through what appears in that stationary image.

Any type of image, drawing, painting, or meme can perform this role of conveying "a thousand words" of meaning. Storytelling is an ancient and fundamental art. When we think of famous works of art, such as Michelangelo's Sistine Chapel ceiling or da Vinci's *Mona Lisa*, part of what makes them so famous is their ability to evoke stories, questions, and feelings in their viewers.

While every form of art is connected to storytelling, photography is uniquely associated with this function. You can probably think of examples of photographs that are particularly compelling and which conjure an entire story in your mind. They may be famous images like *Raising the Flag on Iwo Jima* that help a public audience connect with a significant moment in history. Alternatively, you may think of personal images like a favorite photo from a family vacation that conveys a strong sense of the whole experience and setting.

Photography that actively seeks to tell a story is called *narrative photography*. A photograph that captures a single moment in time can nonetheless convey meaning that transcends that single moment. A subtype of narrative photography is photojournalism. This is photography that is specifically intended to tell a news story, and you can find great examples in nearly any major newspaper.

# CREATING A NARRATIVE

At its foundation, a narrative is simply a story. We often associate narratives with spoken or written communication. For example, think of the word *narrator*, which refers to the person providing a spoken narrative. However, a narrative doesn't necessarily need to be captured in words. A great deal of photography conveys a narrative, whether the photographer specifically intended for it to do so or not. By understanding the use and significance of narrative in your photography, you will be able to channel this element of your craft to create meaningful, compelling images.

Traditionally, narratives include several key elements such as an introduction, some type of conflict that emerges, a climax in the story, a resolution, and an ending. It is neither necessary nor likely that you will capture all these storytelling elements in a single photograph. However, planning a photo at a key moment in the story can help draw viewers in, making them wonder about what came before and after.

A good example of this comes from photojournalism. Imagine a photograph that features two world leaders from countries that have a history of conflict with one another. In the photo, the two world leaders are shaking hands while smiling at the camera. This may be the "resolution" phase of the storytelling arc. Perhaps rounds of heated discussion have led to a happy ending.

If that's the case, viewers of the image may become curious about the content of those discussions and be motivated to read the accompanying news story in detail to figure out how this was achieved. Viewers may also become invested in what will come next: Will this happy relationship last? In this way, through an image that captures just a single moment, a photo can effectively conjure geopolitical histories, diplomacy, and curiosity about the future of this story. That's a lot of rich and complex content embedded within a reader's experience of a single photograph.

There are two main types of narratives that can be captured in narrative photography: constructed narratives and documented narratives. Constructed narratives are those that you have envisioned, chosen, and executed specifically for the purpose of telling this particular story. You can think of these as "staged" narratives. In contrast, documented narratives have this name because you're simply documenting a story or event as it occurs. You haven't "constructed" this story; you are just creating a record that it occurred.

A simple example of this is wedding photography: if you photograph a newly married couple as they're congratulated by family and friends, you are documenting a story as it unfolds. However, if you asked some of your friends to dress up and pretend to get married so that you could take their picture, that would be a constructed narrative.

As you think through your intentions for narrative photography, you first must determine whether your goals are to document moments that are occurring without any intervention from you as the photographer or whether you want to capture images of moments that you have crafted specifically for this purpose. In either case, you will need to ensure your photo captures sufficiently meaningful storytelling elements to get the story across to your viewer.

# CAPTURING EMOTION

Given that most of human communication is nonverbal, you can capture a great deal of understandable human emotion in a single static image. Don't underestimate the power of nuanced facial expressions or gestures. Your viewer will automatically and unconsciously note a slightly raised eyebrow, a worried wrinkle on a forehead, or a tightly balled fist even if it's not in the forefront of the image. Our brains are programmed to seek out these emotional cues when viewing other people and even to look for them in animals. Your job as the photographer is to capture these cues, but you don't need to exaggerate them in order to make sure the viewer will pick up on them.

When photographing a human subject, it's often enough to instruct them to think deeply about a particular emotion. For example, you can tell the subject to think about a time when they felt happy. If your subject follows that instruction and concentrates on an experience that they associate with a strong emotion, the signs of that emotion will become perceptible on their face. This way of prompting your subject is crucial in constructive narratives, as you need to ensure the people you've positioned in the image are conveying the emotion you intend. However, in documented narratives, the genuine emotions of the moment are already present, and your job is to document them on film.

# DOCUMENTING MOMENTS

When you set out to document a particular moment in your photography, whether it's an event, natural phenomenon, or fleeting emotion across someone's face, your goal is likely to capture that moment's core essence as accurately as possible. Doing so represents the culmination of what you have learned so far in this book. You will need to be prepared to work quickly, capturing quick shifts in movement and emotion, while ensuring that your lighting and composition serve to showcase the story of the moment. This comes down to planning, skill, and, inevitably, a little bit of luck.

You have the most control when photographing constructed moments. In theory, you have the ability to choose and organize an optimal setting and lighting to suit your purposes. However, when photographing in less predictable settings, you must be prepared to adjust to changes in weather, unexpected lighting and shadows, and the possibility that you will not be able to get as close to the subject as you may like. Be prepared with equipment that will allow you to quickly adapt.

Most importantly, know your goals in advance. What is your priority when documenting this moment? Is it to showcase the full range of people involved or to give viewers a sense of scale and grandeur? Is it to highlight an intimate, fleeting emotion experienced by just one person? By knowing your goals and keeping them at the forefront of your mind when you set out to document a moment, you will be more likely to stay on track rather than be distracted by the other elements of your surroundings.

# [15]
# CANDID STREET PHOTOGRAPHY

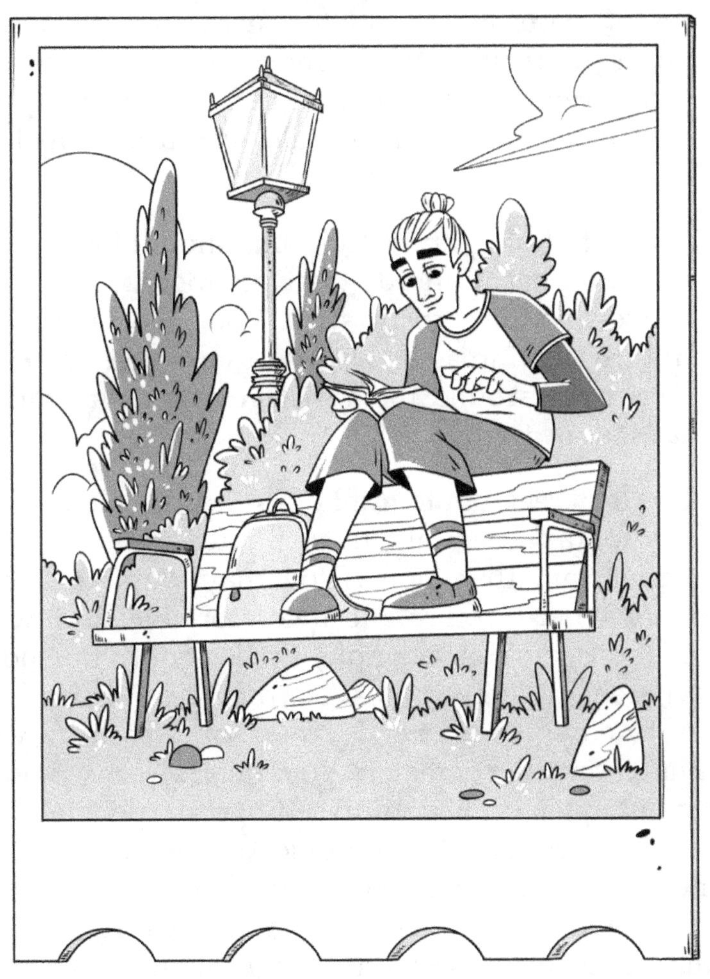

Earlier in this book, we discussed candid photography, which stands in opposition to posed or portrait photography. We also discussed the importance of setting and landscape in photography. This next section on candid street photography brings those elements together to focus on un-posed, natural photographs, especially in urban or semi-urban environments.

The internet and style magazines are full of candid street photography, as this is the nature of paparazzi photography. These types of shots are meant to capture people living their authentic lives in their natural environments. However, some planning and preparation goes into candid street photography even though the end result should capture a real, human moment.

As in any candid photography, the focus should be on the subject and the photographer. Candid street photography captures and conveys a mood and an artistic style. Your choice of whom and what to capture in an image, and the environment or mood that you seek to convey around them, will reveal just as much about you as what's in the frame.

Your task as a street photographer is simple: Find interesting things to photograph and take those photos well. Of course, this is much easier said than done. You may want to start in the environments where you're most comfortable and which are most familiar to you. For example, think about your hometown or a city where you've lived most of your life. This is a place you know how to navigate efficiently, and you also have your own sense of its essential character. You may already know some interesting, unique, or beautiful settings or people there that could provide good photographic subjects. This familiar environment is where you will want to hone your street-photography skills. Only then might you want to tackle bigger, less familiar environments as a street photographer.

# BLENDING IN

One key to being an effective candid photographer is that the image should suggest that you, the photographer, are not actually there. These images should not convey any sense of being posed or prepped for the camera. Instead, you want to capture people in their natural environments, performing any actions or behaviors they otherwise would be if you weren't present. You are documenting these moments rather than constructing them.

As a street photographer, you'll need to blend in with your environment. If you are carrying large equipment and bulky lenses around on the sidewalk, people will immediately identify you as a photographer. They may be curious and want their picture taken, thinking they'll show up in a magazine or online. Others will be nervous and avoidant, worried about those same outcomes.

In either case, whether you are welcomed or rebuffed, the behavior of the people around you is impacted directly by your presence. You would no longer be taking a picture of their authentic selves in the day. Instead, you would be documenting their reactions to you and your equipment. This is not likely to be your goal in these settings.

When setting out for a street photography session, travel light. Choose a camera that's inconspicuous, and dress to blend in. Don't yell to your subjects or otherwise call attention to yourself. Most importantly, don't make eye contact with those you intend to photograph, as that's likely to call their attention and distract them from whatever they were doing. Try to be present but not noticeable so that you can best observe and capture what's going on around you.

Another technique is to keep your camera up for longer than you normally would. When pursuing photography, you may typically keep the camera down until you're ready to shoot a picture, put it up to your eye for that purpose, and then immediately lower it again. However, this camera-up, camera-down activity is recognizable to others, creating an unnecessary distraction. By keeping your camera at your eye for longer periods, you can reduce that recognizable and distracting motion.

# ETHICAL CONSIDERATIONS

The need to effectively blend in with your surroundings to capture authentic images of daily life is directly offset by the ethical considerations and respect you owe to your subjects as a photographer. While images taken without the knowledge or express approval of a subject can seem the most authentic, this must be balanced by the subject's rights and their possible desire not to be photographed. Ethical considerations will be discussed in greater detail later in this book. However, they deserve a mention here as they relate to street photography, which involves images of strangers by definition.

Photographers have an ethical responsibility to show a degree of respect to their subjects, and this includes those subjects' desire for and right to privacy. The right to privacy is a matter of law, not of opinion. While it is usually legal to photograph someone without their express consent, this can depend on the location and context. Double check privacy laws before beginning street photography, as they can vary by location.

# FRAMING EVERYDAY SCENES

When it comes to street photography, framing can be especially important and a uniquely meaningful way to capture a sense of

100

place and time. When you use elements of the surrounding environment to frame your image, you are not only executing an effective composition, but the inclusion of those elements also helps enrich the viewer's understanding of the environment.

For example, street photography in Manhattan is most naturally framed by tall buildings, subway signs, or lines of traffic. These are effective framing elements, but they also directly and powerfully convey a recognizable sense of place, enriching your image both in its structure and meaning.

Candid street photography captured in a coastal town may be framed by the sand of the beach, a long boardwalk, or surfers carrying their boards. Every locale features recognizable elements that add to its personality and sense of place. Look for geometric elements in the built environment or interesting patterns to include within your frame. This context is essential to effective street photography. Without that sense of place, your images are more like portraits than true street photography. The latter depends upon its authentic sense of an environment and the people and things found within it.

# [16]
# WILDLIFE PHOTOGRAPHY TECHNIQUES

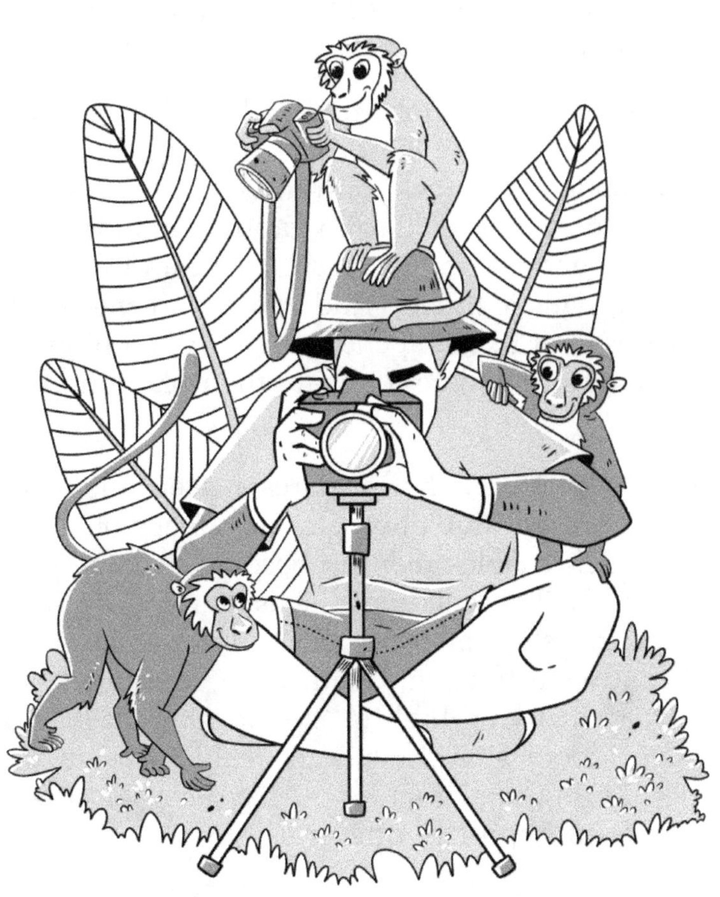

At its foundation, wildlife photography shares much in common with street photography; the idea is to capture living beings performing their natural behaviors in their natural habitats. However, since your primary subject in wildlife photography is just that—wildlife—and the habitat is likely to be a natural rather than built one, your techniques, aims, and specific considerations will be quite different.

Publications like *National Geographic* provide rich inspiration for aspiring wildlife photographers. Beautiful, engaging images of animals are popular across divisions of culture and age, making this genre of photography an enduring and global one.

The same general rules apply to wildlife photography as any other area of photography: Prioritize lighting, be prepared for your environment, and know your goals in advance. The golden hour is an optimal time of day to capture luminous images of wildlife, but depending on the species you aim to photograph, it might not be a realistic time to find subjects. If the creatures you seek are nocturnal or like to spend their early mornings snoozing, you'll have to accommodate for that when planning your photo sessions.

Being a wildlife photographer requires a deep understanding of your subject. Some wildlife photographers focus on a few species or habitats, which enables them to become deeply familiar with their subjects' daily schedules. This familiarity allows the photographer to better plan for their photo shoot by knowing where to be, at what time, and with what equipment. Will birds be very active and flying high in the morning? If so, you might need a longer zoom lens. If they're likely to be in their nests feeding their young, make sure you have chosen a fast shutter speed to capture the animals' quick movements.

Taking the time to research the animals you hope to photograph in advance will make all the difference between a successful photo session and a disappointing one.

# PATIENCE AND OBSERVATION

Photography always requires patience regardless of your setting or subject. Photo sessions may be tedious, and the editing process can be laborious. However, patience is especially critical for wildlife photographers. Wild animals cannot be put on a schedule and will not perform for the camera on cue. Rather than trying to overly predict or control a photo session, wildlife photographers must observe and wait, hoping to gain enough clues into an animal's behavior to eventually capture that winning shot.

Given this fact, you should never head into wildlife photography underprepared. While you want to travel light, you should always bring along water and a light snack in case you end up waiting a long time for your subject to emerge.

Your ability to work quietly and without undue distraction in nature is referred to as your *fieldcraft skill*. By building up your fieldcraft skills, you'll be able to move in a natural environment while creating as little disturbance as possible. This is important for a wildlife photographer because a disturbance will usually cause animals to run away from you. With strong fieldcraft skills, you will be better able to approach and observe animals without scaring them away, giving you more time and opportunity to frame and capture your shot.

Even with a strong knowledge of the animals you intend to photograph and excellent fieldcraft skills, every wildlife photographer has some days that are unsuccessful. Returning to the same place day after day is a necessary element of this genre of photography. Doing so will further help the animals get used to your presence and give you more opportunity to learn their habits, a time-consuming investment that will be worthwhile in the end.

# CAMERA SETTINGS
# FOR WILDLIFE

Wildlife photography presents many specific challenges given its subject matter. One of these is the fact that your wild animals are unlikely to remain still for long periods or deliver the angles and poses that photographers might prefer. Keeping up with a moving subject presents a major challenge in photography.

Another challenge specific to wildlife photography is natural light, especially since many animals are active at night, dawn, and dusk. You may often be working in conditions of low light while trying to capture the perfect wildlife images.

In general, you should plan to use faster shutter speeds when photographing wildlife. Experiment with shutter speeds of 1/250th of a second and higher. This fast shutter speed will allow you to effectively capture movement without significant blur in the image.

Unsurprisingly, you will likely use a larger aperture to make up for low natural light levels during many wildlife photography sessions. If you're photographing a subject at night, you'll need to use every tool at your disposal to ensure that enough light is captured by the camera to create a clear image. Use wide apertures in dimly lit settings, and when you do, remember that this will also result in a narrower depth of field.

Finally, you will want to be thoughtful about the ISO setting you use on your camera. While increasing ISO value will brighten your photos, and therefore may seem desirable in many wildlife photography sessions, doing so will also result in grainy photos. You will need to find the right balance between brightness and clarity to produce high-quality images. This typically means an ISO between 100 and 800. Some new cameras continue to produce clear images even beyond ISO 800. Take some experimental photos with your camera so that you know what to expect in terms of output at different ISO values and you can plan your photo shoot accordingly.

# UNDERSTANDING ANIMAL BEHAVIOR

As stated earlier, a wildlife photographer must have a basic understanding of the behaviors and habits of the animal species they intend to photograph. This knowledge allows the photographer to plan effectively for their photos, predicting where and when the animals will appear, and positioning themselves strategically to capture clear images.

Beyond that general information, many wildlife photographers gain a much more detailed understanding of their species of interest over time. By learning the nuances of an animal's behavior patterns, you can become much more likely to capture the perfect image. While these details depend entirely on the species and habitat, we will present some general tips on animal behavior that you may find helpful as you begin to explore wildlife photography.

Many photographers seek to capture images of animals at the instant they transition from being stationary to on the move. This is a dynamic moment that can create an engaging, impactful image. However, it is an extremely challenging moment to capture, as the transition from stillness to motion occurs in a fraction of a second. A nuanced knowledge of animal behavior can help with this. For example, birds lean forward slightly in the moments before they take flight. By being alert to that tiny characteristic movement, you can predict that flight is about to occur. Even that tiny bit of warning can make the difference between capturing the key moment and missing it.

Over time, you may become alert to signs of fear or stress in animals, which you can work to avoid, as they may hint at poor fieldcraft skills. For example, an owl will slightly widen its eyes when stressed. If you see this occur, it may suggest the owl is about to fly away, so your time to capture a photo is limited. In contrast, animals typically engage in grooming and napping only when they are relaxed. This suggests you have a bit more time to work on capturing the perfect image.

Read books about the behavior of the animals you hope to photograph and watch videos on reputable wildlife sites online. The more you observe and learn about their behavior, the better you'll be able to capture images that fully embody them.

# SAFETY GUIDELINES

Wildlife photography can take you to some dramatic and fascinating settings. These settings may also be remote, slippery, steep, or otherwise risky for humans. It's essential that you prepare effectively for the environments you will encounter and that you follow some general safety guidelines when pursuing wildlife photography.

First, know and follow all posted rules and regulations for the land where you are photographing. For example, if you are in a national park, you'll have access to a wide array of fascinating wildlife. However, you must also stay on marked trails and avoid crossing over any fences or other barriers. If you hope to take close-up photos of animals, you can accomplish this using zoom lenses rather than trying to approach the animal. Back away from an animal as needed to maintain a safe distance.

Always notify others of your intended location and itinerary for a photography session. It's also a good idea to carry a basic first aid kit whenever you're out in the wilderness. Your kit should include some basic bandages, antiseptic ointment, and something to use as a tourniquet if needed.

Dress appropriately for your environment, especially when it comes to your footwear. Sturdy shoes with good traction and stable soles are essential for walking outdoors on uncertain terrain or in wet conditions. While you want to wear colors that will help you blend in with your environment, make sure they provide the sun or rain protection you need for the climate.

While we all know to be afraid of large animals like bears or wolves, don't underestimate the potential dangers of smaller animals. Any animal can pose a threat when it's scared or perceives you as a danger to its young.

# [17]
# LONG EXPOSURE MAGIC

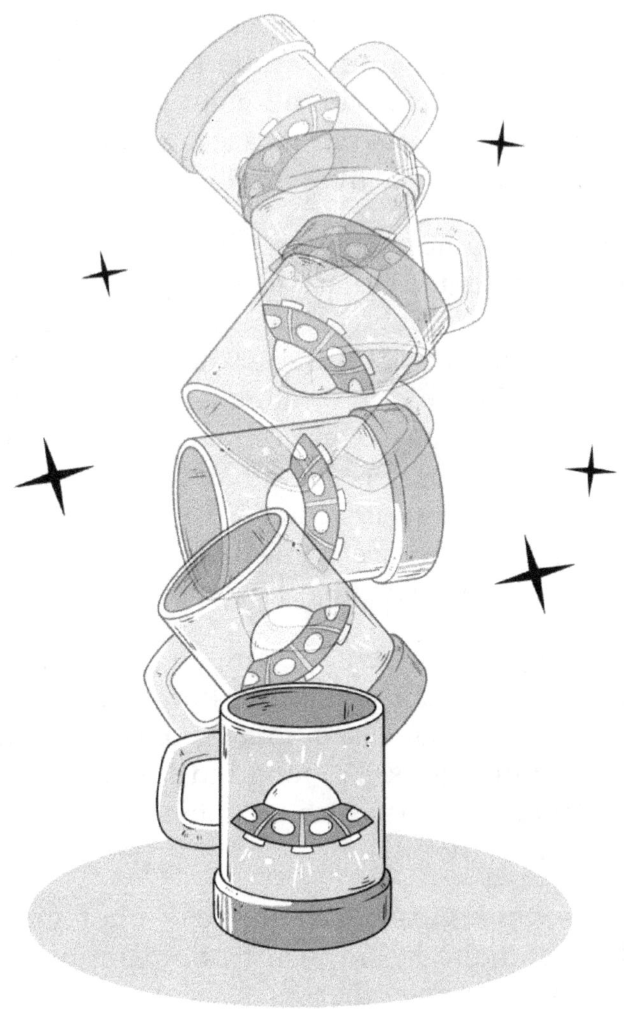

The previous section highlighted techniques for wildlife photography, which is often about using fast shutter speeds to capture subjects in motion. Next, we will turn our attention to quite a different challenge: maximizing the potential of long exposures to convey a sense of movement and the passage of time.

Long-exposure photography refers to capturing a single image over an extended period of time. This technique works best when you can focus on a stationary subject, such as a boulder, while allowing elements in the frame around it to continue moving. You will capture the image with a longer shutter speed, and the resulting effect will be a subject that's clear with its surroundings somewhat blurred to convey their motion.

A "long" exposure time is not specifically defined. Instead, a photograph is considered to have a long exposure when the shutter speed was too slow to capture an image that's sharp throughout. Instead, it has captured some motion, which appears as softness or blur. When done well, long-exposure photography creates compelling images that embody both stillness and motion, expressing a sense of time passing for the viewer despite the fact that the photo itself is static. Use long exposure times when you intend to capture some blur or the appearance of softness surrounding a clear subject in your images.

You've undoubtedly seen examples of long-exposure photography before even if you didn't know how it was created. For example, you may have seen images of cars driving at night where all the taillights look like long red lines. You may be able to think of a landscape in which all the clouds appeared to be stretched long across the sky.

Long exposures can be used for a range of photography genres. It's a popular technique in landscape photography as well as in street photography, among others.

# CAPTURING MOTION

One of the primary reasons to use long exposures is to capture motion. While a photograph is ultimately a still image, by allowing your shutter to remain open, any moving elements within the photograph will appear blurred. This blurring allows them to impart a sense of motion even within a static image.

While this isn't a definitive rule, some photographers argue that long exposure works best to convey motion when only some elements in the image are in motion and at least one is completely static. The static element, such as a tree in the background, will appear crisply focused in the image, which emphasizes the dynamic effect of other elements whose movement is conveyed through blur. Incorporating static elements also provides your image with a sense of structure and framing, which isn't as easily achieved when all objects in the photo are in motion.

In order to achieve that crisp focus for static elements in your photo, you will likely need to use a tripod to ensure the camera is completely still during the long exposure.

# ACHIEVING LIGHT TRAILS

Light trails result from light sources in motion across the frame of an image taken with long exposure. The magic of light trails is that they don't actually exist in real life. The camera is able to capture an optical effect, creating a visual that everyone can recognize despite not having seen it firsthand in a natural environment.

Light trails are often captured most effectively in low-light situations, especially at sunset. The lower environmental light allows your moving light source to become the focus of the image and create that characteristic trail of color across the frame. While traffic and roadways are the most common sources of light trails in photography, they are not your only options. You can create light trails from photographing stationary streetlights while you're a passenger in a moving vehicle or even from having a friend manually move a flashlight through the air while you take pictures. This technique is called *light painting*.

Light trails tend to be captured best between shutter speeds of 5 and 60 seconds, depending on the source and speed of the moving light. It may take time and patience to master your light-trail photography. To maximize your chances of success, aim for that evening sunset hour for taking these pictures, and as with any long-exposure techniques, be sure to bring your tripod.

# CREATING DREAMY WATER EFFECTS

It's possible to create beautifully textured images of water using long exposures of approximately 15 to 30 seconds. When done effectively, the surface of the water can take on a soft, velvety appearance or even become cloud-like and hazy.

When aiming for that foggy-water effect, you need two main ingredients: a moving body of water and stationary elements in or around the water. These may take the form of waves rushing in between rocks along a beach, a stream meandering past tree roots, or water at the edge of a lake lapping the sand. Waterfalls provide an especially beautiful subject for this type of photography. When done well, the waterfall assumes a dreamy look that exudes calm and relaxation.

You may remember from earlier in this book that an ND filter is a neutral density filter. ND filters reduce noise in images. They're optimal for long exposures, especially for capturing water effects. You can experiment with 3-stop, 6-stop, and 10-stop ND filters to determine their unique effects and utility.

# [18]
# MASTERING PORTRAIT LIGHTING

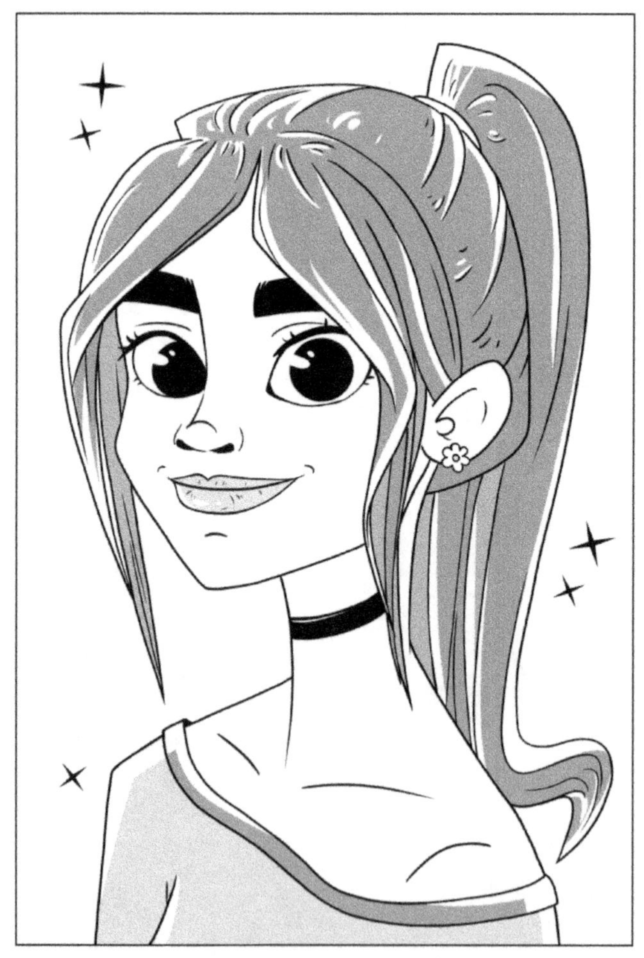

Appropriate lighting is essential when you're pursuing portraiture. There are many different approaches to portrait lighting depending on the effect you intend to create, and this chapter will cover several of your options.

Portrait photography, by definition, is focused on a particular subject, usually a human subject. In general, when a person sits for a portrait, they do so with the hope that the result will be flattering to them. They may hope to look their best, whatever that means to them, or want certain elements of their personality or style to shine through. Using lighting strategically in your portrait sessions is one of the most important ways to ensure that these goals are met.

When embarking on a portrait session with a new client or subject, take time to discuss their goals and your intentions prior to taking any photos. You as the photographer should be aware of the subject's hopes for this photograph, as well as their insecurities or aspects of the photo session that make them nervous. With this information in mind, you can adjust facets of your lighting—the angles at which light hits the subject, the lighting equipment you may or may not use, and the amount of light overall that will appear in your image—to accentuate or conceal elements as needed.

In portrait photography, you will be focusing on the lighting pattern, which is the way the light falls across your subject's face to create some areas of light and some of shadow. As you can imagine, deep shadows need to be carefully controlled in portrait photography, lest they distort or obscure your subject's features.

An essential feature of portrait photography is the catchlight, or the small spot of light that should appear in the subject's eye in the final image. The catchlight can come from either natural or artificial lighting that is placed directly in front of the subject. If you can't see it before snapping the shutter, ask your subject to tilt or rotate their head very slightly until it appears.

# STUDIO LIGHTING

Formal and professional portrait photography often take place in a studio, which is a closed environment that allows the photographer total control over lighting and background. While there are typically less distractions in a studio, if the subject is a baby or young child, you might intentionally incorporate some entertaining distractions.

In a studio, much of the heavy lifting in terms of lighting will be done by a key light. This is the main light source for your photo. Manipulating the placement and angle of the key light will allow you to achieve several classic lighting effects for portraits.

Using your key light, you have a few options. Two standard effects to know are called *broad lighting* and *short lighting*. Picture your subject seated in front of you with their head turned slightly at an angle so that you can see one full side of their nose but not the full other side. *Broad lighting* refers to the light landing first on the side of the face that is closer to you, illuminating the full side that you can see. *Short lighting* refers to the light landing first on the other side of the person's face, the side slightly angled away from you, leaving the side facing you slightly in shadow.

Alternatively, you may consider butterfly lighting where the subject sits facing straight on to the camera and the key light is positioned up higher than the subject's eye level. The key light will need to be angled down somewhat to point at the subject, and the resulting image will have a small butterfly-shaped shadow under the person's nose. This shadow is what gives this lighting style its name.

Loop lighting is achieved by combining short lighting with butterfly lighting: a high, down-angled key light that catches the far side of the subject's face. Loop lighting is often used in professional headshots. If the key light is moved even higher, and even further from the subject, the result will be Rembrandt lighting, which is defined by a long shadow from the nose that connects to the part of the cheek that's in shadow. As its name suggests, this style of portrait lighting has a more dramatic effect than its loop-lighting counterpart. By turning the subject's face perpendicular to the camera and using your key light to illuminate only the edge or outline of their profile, you can achieve a dramatic profile light.

Each of these approaches to portrait lighting will showcase different features of your subject, and each creates a different mood. For something formal or professional, you may want to consider butterfly or loop lighting. More dramatic goals may best be achieved by Rembrandt, profile, or short lighting.

# NATURAL LIGHT PORTRAITS

While the above lighting tips all take place in a studio with lighting equipment, this doesn't mean that these highly controlled environments are the only ones suited to portraiture. It's entirely possible to take excellent portraits using only natural light as long as you're strategic about timing and well attuned to the direction and strength of the light around you.

It's generally not advisable to attempt portrait photography under direct midday sun. This leads to dramatic shadows and a risk of overexposure, as discussed earlier. If you have to shoot at midday, opt for bright shade instead of direct sun. In this setting, you can benefit from bright ambient lighting but in a softer form that's easier to work with. For example, position your subjects under a dense tree or just a few feet inside an open doorway on a bright day. This combination of soft shade in a bright environment can create very flattering portraits. The golden hour is also a great option for portraiture in natural light.

You can use the lighting effects described above in a natural setting, assuming the sun plays the role of your key light. Position your subject for broad, short, or even butterfly lighting in relation to the sun. However, be careful to avoid any position that has your subject facing directly into the sun, as they will likely need to squint, and the lighting will be overly harsh and unflattering for most people.

# USING REFLECTORS AND DIFFUSERS

Reflectors and diffusers are extremely useful tools in portrait photography. Reflectors and diffusers can both be used in either studio or natural light settings, though diffusers are more commonly used with artificial lighting.

A reflector is, as its name suggests, a highly reflective object that will bounce light off its surface and back at your subject. You can use reflectors to change the direction of light in an image, such as to illuminate the side of a subject's face that's turned away from the light source. In many cases, a reflector can effectively serve as an additional light source. While it doesn't create its own light, its ability to reflect light from other sources gives you a great deal of control over the location and intensity of light in your photos.

A diffuser serves a very different purpose. A diffuser is made of thin, white material that can be placed in front of your light source to soften the light's appearance and spread it over a larger area. Diffusers create light that appears softer and often more flattering to your subject. They are generally designed for use with artificial light sources. In addition to their mellowing effects and ability to create a more even appearance, diffusers also create a more comfortable experience for your subject by reducing the harshness of a key light aimed in their direction. If you want to use a diffuser to soften harsh outdoor lighting from the sun, you may find that you need a larger surface area than what's

120

provided by a standard diffuser. Some photographers have success using large white bedsheets for this purpose as they provide the same diffuse lighting effect but with a much larger surface area that is well suited to many outdoor photo shoots.

# [19]
# WORKING
# WITH MODELS

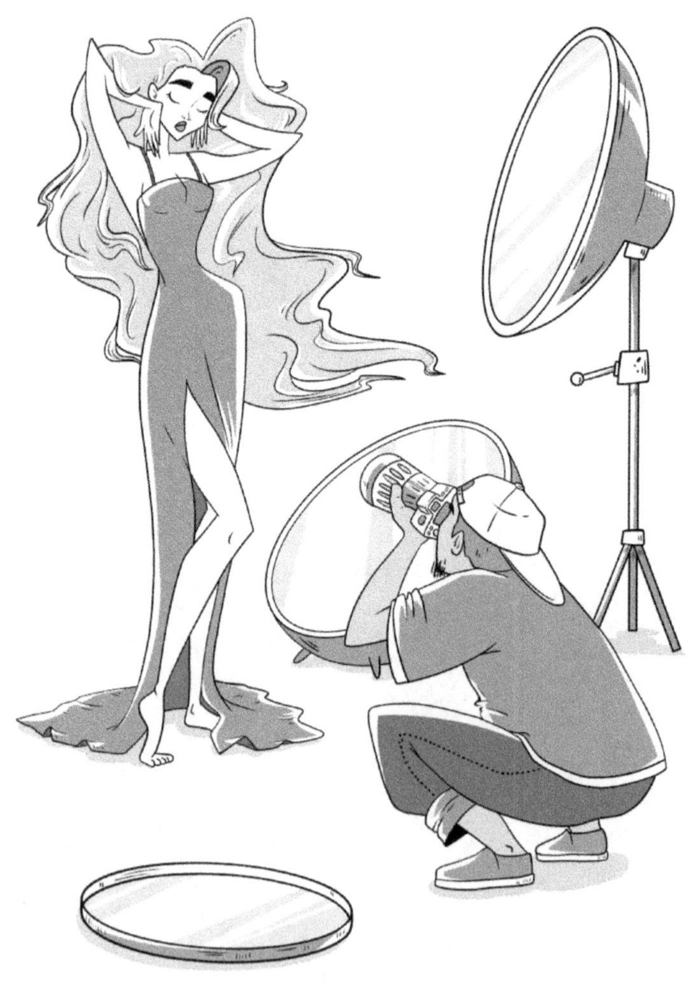

All the aforementioned tips related to portraiture apply equally to family, friends, casual clients, and professional models. You have the same lighting options available to you regardless of the nature of your subject, but working with professional models may open up a wider range of drama and creativity in your photography. This is because a model can serve as a true creative partner in your craft, contributing to the vision for the photo.

If you choose to pursue photography that utilizes models, perhaps for marketing, fashion, or beauty photo shoots, there are a few tips that can help you make a good start. However, just as every photographer is unique, every model has their own personality, preferences, and style. While general professionalism and courtesy always serve as a solid foundation for working with models, each relationship will be different, and some experiences will undoubtedly be more successful than others, just as in any professional relationship.

# COMMUNICATION AND COLLABORATION

To begin, it's essential to recognize that the model is your colleague and a collaborator in the creative process. Discuss your vision and process with a model before beginning a photo shoot. Let them know how you like to work and what to expect throughout the shoot, as well as what you hope to achieve. Ideally, you'll have time to hear the model's thoughts and suggestions for the shoot as well. Particularly for newer photographers, the model may have significantly more experience with these types of photographs and may have a good idea of what does and doesn't work well.

Check in with the model throughout the photo shoot to ensure their comfort. While it may look easy, modeling can be physically demanding and very tiring, so be sure to account for breaks during any lengthy photo shoot.

One of the most enjoyable parts of working with a model can be active communication with them throughout the shoot. The model and the photographer are a true partnership, and each must be in tune with the other to achieve a successful shot. Communicate what's working and what isn't and encourage the model to do the same throughout the shoot.

# POSING AND DIRECTING

Some professional photo shoots may have an artistic director or another person who's there to oversee and direct the event. In that case, both the photographer and the model must be in close communication with that person to ensure everyone's intentions are aligned. If a shoot doesn't have an assigned director, then typically the photographer plays that role. Using all the knowledge and skills discussed thus far, you must create a vision for the shoot and then clearly communicate that vision.

In simple terms, this means telling the model what to do, how to pose, and where to look in order to capture the image you're seeking. However, the process is rarely quite as simple as that. Sometimes, the human body can't quite achieve the pose you may have in mind, or perhaps they can't hold it long enough to capture the shot. Maybe it's already been a long day in the elements and your model is fatigued. As in any other partnership, it's through clear and respectful communication that you are most likely to maintain a sense of trust that will see you through to your goal.

Communicate your needs and wants clearly to the model and do so in terms that are respectful. Be sure to use very clear language and be as specific as you can. For example, don't say, "Raise your arm higher," which is vague and will lead to confusion and frustration. Instead, say, "Raise your right arm up about two inches so that your elbow is parallel with your right shoulder and your palm is still facing forward." This level of clarity in your instruction will ensure that no time is wasted, and everyone is on the same page.

In order to provide this level of specificity in your direction, you need to have a clear understanding of your own plans for the shoot in advance. If you intend to be less structured and experiment during the shoot, communicate that to your model so they know what to expect. They may be happy to join in the experimentation as a collaborator.

# BUILDING A PORTFOLIO

If you hope to create a business through portraiture or any other type of photography, the most effective way to do so is by creating a stellar portfolio. A portfolio is a collection of your best photos all together in one place that you can showcase online or share with potential clients. The purpose of a portfolio is to show off what you can do and convince clients to hire you on the basis of the skills on display in the portfolio images.

With landscape photography or other genres that don't require a human subject, you will build your portfolio over time as you take more and more photos. Choose your favorites, and ones that illustrate the full range of your abilities across various locations, lighting strategies, distances, and themes.

However, if you're building a portfolio of portraiture, you will need to be collaborative in your approach. You may be able to start a portfolio that features images of family members and friends who are happy to pose for you as a favor so that you can practice your craft. As your skills develop, you may start offering free or heavily discounted photo sessions to clients. This is a win-win situation that allows you to develop your portfolio, while they get a free or low-cost professional portrait.

Typically, a photography portfolio contains between 12 and 25 images, but there is plenty of variation in this number. Most portfolios nowadays are hosted on online platforms where you can continuously swap out older photographs for newer ones. Make sure you have a portable version of your portfolio as well, whether in hard copy or on a mobile tablet, so that you can show your work to potential clients on the go.

# [20]
# ETHICAL CONSIDERATIONS IN PHOTOGRAPHY

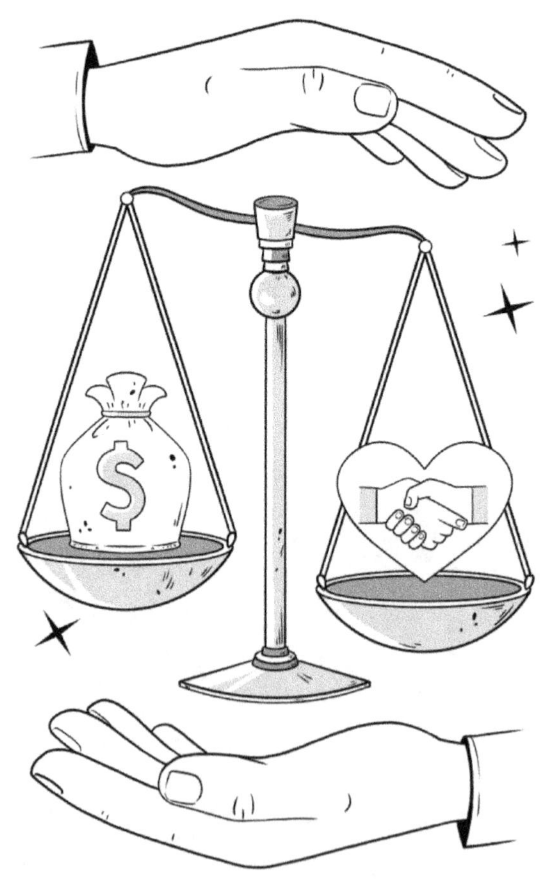

At its heart, photography is about the artistic vision of the photographer, and it's the photographer who exercises control over and ownership of their images in most cases. However, this doesn't mean that the photographer is the only individual whose rights and preferences matter. The ethical issues in this field extend to subject privacy, compensation, narrative creation, and photo manipulation. All are important to consider before you embark upon your photographic journey.

# PRIVACY CONCERNS

The most commonly raised ethical issues in photography relate to the rights of human subjects and especially their right to—or desire for—privacy. In most places, it's legal to take a photograph of a person without their express consent or knowledge. A photographer is within their rights to prioritize blending in and capturing images as they see them. This right extends to public places and anywhere a subject couldn't reasonably expect privacy. However, in general, you shouldn't (or sometimes are not legally allowed to) photograph security personnel, police officers, and government buildings. It's also illegal to photograph someone in a situation where they can reasonably expect privacy such as inside their home.

Even if your photography is entirely legal, you still may encounter a subject who states that they don't wish to be photographed. In this case, it's best to communicate. Stay calm and try to diffuse any tension. You can explain that you're a photographer working on a project and offer to share the image you took of them. Offering a compliment or explanation of your photo can also be helpful. Share something with them like, "I just loved the way the sun was shining on your hair," or "Your sense of style really inspired me, and I wanted to capture it." By explaining your purpose, remaining calm and open, and engaging in conversation, you may be able to smooth over any discomfort.

If your subject remains upset after you've tried to discuss the situation with them, you may choose to delete the image you've taken of them, or you may choose to keep it. You are technically within your rights to do either, according to your own sense of ethics. When in doubt, it's best to delete the image. If you keep it, you will be stuck with an image that you know made someone feel angry or violated, and that will not be a pleasant reminder each time you view it.

# RESPECTS FOR SUBJECTS

In addition to privacy concerns, an ethical photographer will be mindful of their subjects when it comes to issues like context and narratives. *Context* refers to the situation in which you are capturing a photograph. Refrain from intruding upon deep or vulnerable moments without express consent from your subjects. Most photographers also avoid photographing babies and children unless they have received permission from their parents or guardians. These are simple matters of respect and humanity, and any photographer would do well to honor them.

Additionally, as discussed throughout this book, photographs can convey stories and create deep and lasting impressions. This is a great position of power for the photographer, but it's also one of responsibility. When photographing events, places, or people, be mindful of the story that your images will tell. Ask yourself, "Am I showing the truth of this situation? Am I showing both sides of the story? Will I likely perpetuate falsehoods or mistaken assumptions by sharing this photograph?" While every individual's unique reactions to a photograph are beyond the photographer's ability to control or even predict, it's unethical to knowingly craft a misleading impression. Seek to add context to your photographs and illuminate full stories rather than perpetuating narrow views, or half-truths, and avoid taking photographs for the sole purpose of creating controversy.

# PHOTO MANIPULATION ETHICS

This book has already discussed the ways in which you can use post-processing to enhance or alter photographs, often for good reason and with positive intent. It's okay to manipulate your photographs as long as that manipulation or editing is clearly disclosed. It's unethical to pass off an edited photograph as an unedited one.

Photographs should not be used to convince viewers they have seen something that's not actually real, and there have been some harrowing examples of this as far back as several decades ago. While not a new phenomenon, the rise of more complex technologies including AI make it easier than ever to alter photos. However, even subtle changes can quickly become misleading. When you do make use of post-processing options to modify an image, make sure that you indicate clearly that you have done so.

Many professional associations in photography have developed new codes of ethics that seek to address ever-changing technologies and photo-enhancement options. Seek out these codes, or better yet join the associations, so that you can keep up to date on best ethical practices in this field.

# CONCLUSION

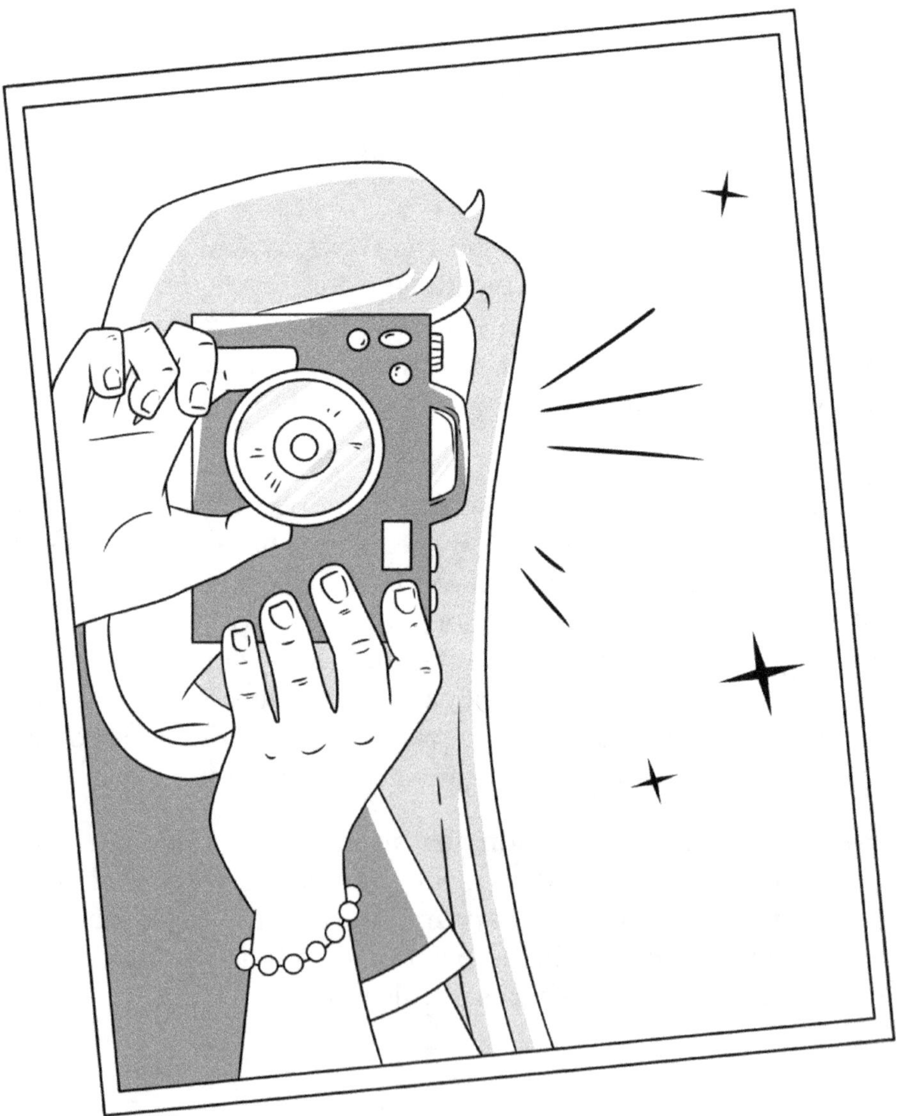

Photography is an art form that can be exciting or calming, inspiring or meditative. Its subjects can be serious or whimsical, realistic or utterly imaginative. Let this diversity be your inspiration as you develop and refine your skills. There's no end to learning photography, no point at which a photographer can announce that they've mastered every subject and technique. This is what makes the art and science of photography a lifelong passion for so many photographers: the endless challenges to pursue.

Whenever you feel that you've gotten into a rut with your photography and you're lacking inspiration, consider a trip to a museum or gallery where you can view the works of others. Pay attention to the details in their images. How have they handled light? How did they achieve that motion effect? What kind of lens did they use to capture that image? By focusing on these details, you may find a new source of inspiration.

When you feel that you have done as much as you can or as much as you want to in one genre, feel free to change it up and try something new. For example, if you've been taking portraits for a long time, maybe it's time to practice your long-exposure landscape photography. Even if they're just for your own edification and enjoyment, building separate portfolios across a range of photographic genres can prove an engaging challenge that keeps a photographer motivated.

This book has provided an introduction for beginners, and with the information contained here, you're in a great position to build a solid set of skills. However, continuing to educate yourself about photographic techniques, post-production options, and new ethical considerations will be an ongoing process. Professional associations for photographers are one of the best ways to keep up with your continuing education, as are local photography clubs. Check community colleges and art schools in your area for classes offered to the public; you might be pleasantly surprised by inspiring offerings and the chance to connect with others who share your interest in photography. In addition, you can find a wealth of online classes—both free and paid—that will help you further develop your skills as a photographer.

One of the best ways to keep up your learning is to find a photography mentor, someone who has been practicing photography for a long time and is happy to share the benefit of their experience with you. Reach out to professional photographers in your area and ask whether you can shadow them for a day, as this can provide a terrific experience to learn from someone else's style.

The more you practice photography, the more you'll develop your own unique style. You'll discover your favorite techniques, tools, and settings as you gain experience. You may even have preferred subjects and color palettes that you return to again and again. Some photographers lean into their own bespoke style and craft an oeuvre that is uniquely and identifiably theirs.

In contrast, some photographers love experimentation and find that their style preferences evolve over time or even abruptly change. This adaptability is a strength of its own in photography, one that allows a photographer to continuously modify their skill set.

Whichever approach you have toward photography, take pleasure in each accomplishment, no matter how small. Remember to appreciate your own works of art and celebrate how far you've come in this field over time. This is a craft that can remain with you throughout your life, providing documentation of your growth and evolution from year to year. Photography is an incredible gift to give yourself and a lucky journey to be on. Any hobby or profession that allows you to focus on capturing and sharing beauty and inspiration is a fortuitous one. Take your inspiration from everything and everyone you can, and most importantly, keep on taking photos.